Bridging Universitiy and Corporation

Volume II

Maria Spindler . Eva Maria Bauer

Research Case Studies as Learning Challenges for Leaders and Organisations

verlags
haus
hernals

Bridging University and Corporation, edited by Maria Spindler and Martin Steger, Volume II

The authors, editors, and publisher will not take any legal responsibility for errors or omissions that may be made in this book. The publisher makes no warranty, expressed or implied, regarding the material contained herein.

Copyright © Verlagshaus Hernals, Vienna 2013
All rights reserved.
www.verlagshaus-hernals.at
Picture: „Der Flug des Ginkgo", 2008, M. Ferner, MT auf Arches 375g,
Catalogue raisonné No. 317
Copyright © M. Ferner, www.michael-ferner.at
Typeset: b+R satzstudio, Graz
ISBN 978-3-902744-28-9

TABLE OF CONTENTS

Introduction 13

Maria Spindler . Martin Steger
The scientific methodology of research case studies
Series editors' foreword 15

Silvia Ettl-Huber . Eva Maria Bauer . Michael Roither
From Master's thesis to case study – an approach for challenging
MBA theses 23

Eva Maria Bauer . Silvia Ettl-Huber
Case studies: definition, application, strengths. 27
1   What is a case study? 27
2   The difference between research case studies and teaching cases . 29
3   Application of research case studies 30
4   Strengths of the research case study 31
5   Challenges for the research case study 33

Maria Spindler
Organizations and their Interplay with Leadership for an Uncertain
Future – Seven Principles.. 37
Principle 1: Leadership action is based on observation 38
Principle 2: Communitized observation is the leverage for complex
leadership actions 40
Principle 3: Complex organizations as self-responsible
entities within an uncertain environment......................... 42
Principle 4: Organization seen as self-responsible units and their
relation with their environment.................................. 43
Principle 5: Questioning, scrutinizing and future-oriented
functionality 45
Principle 6: Organizations seen as self-steering transformers
of societal complexity... 48
Principle 7: Leadership capacity as critically dealing with paradoxes
and functionality.. 50
Conclusions: Collaborative leadership learning allows social
sustainability for organizations for an uncertain future......... 51

Table of Contents

Maria Spindler
What leaders can learn through the case study process............. 55
1   Observation and questioning as learning provocations
    for complex systems 55
2   Case studies as opportunities for further adult learning
    for practitioners 59
    2.1 Telling one's own story to challenge oneself 59
    2.2 Systemised learning from the past for the future......... 60
    2.3 The laboratory situation enables transformation.......... 61
3   Research for one's own practice, science and others............ 62
4   Conclusions: Expand the capacity for learning 63

Silvia Ettl-Huber . Eva Maria Bauer
Supervision of students in the case study process – An elaborated
support process for mastering case studies......................... 67
1   The process of finding a subject 69
2   Three seminars on case studies 69
3   Feedback loops for the Master's thesis 71

Astrid Valek
How the concept of the learning organization can be put
into practice 73
1   Introduction and overview.................................... 73
2   Initial situation 74
    2.1 The concept of the learning organization as a vision
         for the Marketing Director's own leadership 74
    2.2 Initial situation of the bank in 2006 75
    2.3 Interpreting urgency and recognizing it as potential
         for change... 76
3   Structural and personnel changes............................ 78
4   The Marketing Director's strategic realignment of the area 79
5   The Marketing Director's concept of leadership – from hierarchy
    to team... 81
6   Visionary move into the future and setback revealed in figures ... 81
7   Delegate leadership to encourage learning about leadership..... 82
8   Encouraging team learning through a positive perspective 83
9   The team's long-term success in the context of the organization .. 83
10 Conducive and protective management attitudes 85
11 Possible scenarios 86
    11.1 Expanding organizational learning 86

11.2 Power, not learning is at the forefront 86
12 Summary of insights 87

Eva Maria Bauer . Andrea Berger
Change while the engine is running – management challenges
during an extensive change process in the public health sector 91
1 Introduction 91
2 Initial situation 92
   2.1 The consolidation of various clinics as a learning
       opportunity for managers 92
   2.2 Legal basis of the organisation 92
3 The consolidation of over twenty clinics into one large health
   services group 93
   3.1 The structure of the clinic holding company in 2004 93
   3.2 2004 – Learning from challenges 94
       3.2.1 Changing management structures step by step 94
       3.2.2 Changing communication step by step 94
       3.2.3 The uncertainty factor in the change process 95
   3.3 2005 – the turning point – first successes in the
       implementation 96
       3.3.1 Adapting the structures: the first fruits are harvested . 96
       3.3.2. The tide turns – the structural changes are perceived
            more and more positively 96
       3.3.3 The changes bear their first fruits – The regional
            managment further reduces the complexity of the
            organisation 97
       3.3.4 The introduction of regional management has a
            positive impact 97
   3.4 2006: Growing and struggling toward a mutual identity – the
       Personnel Department introduces measures 98
       3.4.1 The implementation in detail 99
   3.5 2007: The beginning of a general orientation project 99
       3.5.1 The realisation of the overall concept 100
   3.6 2008: Management structures gain importance 101
       3.6.1 New demands on managers bring change in turn 101
       3.6.2 Further education for managers and a mutual
            management culture as a factor for success 102
       3.6.3 The training modules for managers 103
   3.7 2009: Organisational development in the central holding
       company is further optimised 104

		3.7.1	The new principle of management and accountability logic	104
		3.7.2	The changed management style between 2004 and 2009 is a trend-setter for the further development of the organisation	105
		3.7.3	Subsequent reflection on the change process from the point of view of the managers	106
4	Scenarios for the future			107
	4.1	Positive scenario: "Competition grows, development is spurred"		107
	4.2	Negative scenario: "Loss of power for the central holding company, disintegration of the organisation"		110
	4.3	Recapitulation and reflection on the empirical insights		110

Harald Gansfuss . Maria Spindler
Merger as the motivation for the move from extended workbench
to independent company 113

1	Introduction			113
2	Initial situation			113
	2.1	Overview of the companies involved		113
	2.2	The planned competitive advantage to be obtained through the upward revaluation of the extended workbench		115
	2.3	The complexity of the products, production and customer relations		116
	2.4	Sale and contract design as formation of a cooperation (7/2002–2/2003)		116
	2.5	Evaluation and planning of the requirements for the consolidation of the companies (3–5/2003)		117
3	The creation of solutions (10/2003–12/2006)			118
	3.1	Solution 1: Transfer of knowledge from JERMAN to NOVAK CZECH (10/2003–3/2005)		118
	3.2	Solution 2: Shift in priorities–sales expertise from the market and EDP integration (3/2005–10/2005)		119
		3.2.1	Speed up the hiring of qualified workers in the technicaland sales areas	119
		3.2.2	The acquisition of an integrated EDP system to support operative processes (6/2004– 6/2005)	120
	3.3	Solution 3: Management shifts (9/2005–2/2006)		121
	3.4	Solution 4: The putsch against the Austrian hierarchical system (1/2006–6/2006)		124

    3.5   Solution 5: Slow buildup of independence and complexity
           (from 6/2006) 126
          3.5.1 Buildup of a local Czech area management 126
          3.5.2 Divided responsibility and language training ensure
                development of the complete perspective and an
                information base for all 126
          3.5.3 Quality awareness: management and customer support 128
          3.5.4 Cooperative future-oriented management with
                simultaneous decisive measures (from 8/2006) 128
          3.5.5 Medium-term effects of the establishment of
                independence (2007–2010) 130
4   Scenarios for the future 130
    4.1   Integrative, meaningful forms of cooperation are lost again . 131
    4.2   Cooperation, responsibility and collective learning
           continue to develop 132
5   Summary of interpretation................................ 132

Natasa Ilic, MBA
Institutionalisation and strategic focus of Public Relations (PR) at the
Volksbank Serbia... 137
Introduction 137
1   Initial situation 139
    1.1   The environment: the nation 139
          1.1.1 Serbia in 1999: Hunger, cold, inflation, unemployment 139
          1.1.2. Political and economic turnaround: Serbia on the
                path to the EU............................... 140
2   The organisation – development and strategy 140
    2.1   Challenges to the newly founded bank in a nation
           in transition 140
    2.2   Conclusion: rapid growth = need for redirection 141
3   The path to institutionalised public relations in the Volksbank
    Serbia – what actually happened, and above all, how? 142
    3.1   From PR amateur to PR professional in a newly founded bank 142
    3.2   After the bank was founded, the Marketing Department
           dealt with press relations as needed 143
    3.3   PR activities become the secondary area of responsibility
           of the Assistant to the Executive Board.................. 144
    3.4   Rapid growth in the bank, more need for public relations... 144
    3.5   First signs of organizational establishment: Important course
           setting on the path to institutionalisation of PR 145

3.6 Actions resulting from practice and results of PR work led to the birth of a new organizational area 148
3.7 Changes in the Executive Board bring new perspectives for the institutionalisation of PR 149
3.8 The position of Public Relations Manager was approved: the employee's interests met the bank's needs 150
3.9 Individual development and motivation of an employee and results of the informally carried out PR work 151
3.10 Public Relations as a control function and reputation management: strategic focus of PR in the Volksbank since the end of 2006 152
4 Theoretical embedding 156
   4.1 Social theories: modern society and competition as conditions for professional PR work 156
   4.2 Organization theories: PR as a central function is an achievement of organizational goals 157
   4.3 Definitions of the public, communication and public relations 158
5 Scenarios of the case 159
   5.1 Scenario 1: The tasks of the Marketing and Communications Department grow further and change 159
   5.2 Scenario 2: The importance of professional communication decreases 159
6 Summary of interpretation and conclusions 160

Eva Maria Bauer
From individual learning to organisational learning 163
1 Introduction 163
2 Presentation of results 164
   2.1 Insights into individual learning 164
      2.1.1 The first step of individual learning – choosing a topic 164
      2.1.2 The path to the actual topic – support from the organisation 165
      2.1.3 A practical case becomes academic – structuring as a task 165
      2.1.4 The challenge of writing a case study – significant identification of new perspectives 166
      2.1.5 The "easy" parts of a case study – generating opportunities for learning 167

		2.1.6	Learning through difficulties in writing a case study – questioning one's own competence and changing management structures	167
		2.1.7	Individual learning through precise observation of management decisions	168
		2.1.8	Consequences of the case study for personal development	169
	2.2	Insights into organisational learning		169
		2.2.1	The importance of the organisation in the case study – the support of the organisation as a condition for the success of a case study	169
		2.2.2	The path to organisational learning – consequences of the case study for the organisation	170
		2.2.3	Learning by the organisations from the case studies	170
		2.2.4	The path to implementation in the organisations	171
3	Discussion and interpretation of the results			171
About the Authors				175

INTRODUCTION

This book emerged from our experience of the last six years. We developed a vast number of concepts, material and frameworks, received positive and enlightening feedback from students, worked hard and developed a lot about adult learning. It was a joint effort that made this success possible. It is a book by practitioners for practitioners. It represents a milestone: on the one hand, the conclusion of a six-year development and learning process and on the other hand, the beginning of an extensive institutionalisation. The joint effort flowed from various perspectives and backgrounds into this book in the form of

- Scientific and strategic frameworks
- Theoretical implementations and methodical developments
- Empirical presentations.

The results define a possible path for the requirements of learning through an academic thesis. The vision of facilitating a meaningful activity for those involved, leading to the case study as a product, guided our actions. It transcends the cliché, "I am writing this academic thesis in order to obtain an MBA."

Master's theses based on case studies demand a higher level of reflective learning about the authors' situations: based on their burning questions about taking their own practice as the starting point and questioning it again and again; telling the stories of their own professional actions and transforming them into academic papers; overcoming their own blind spots through feedback and critical questioning – this accommodates within the practitioners' studies the complete body of their underlying experience. Each is the expert and learner for his or her leadership situation. University learning thus becomes the basis for personal leadership development in interplay with organisational context. Our conception is that this personal learning through the Master's thesis also activates long-term corporate learning.

This type of research case study meets the requirement of generating empirical, scientifically exploitable data for the following target groups:

- Leaders
- Corporations
- Post-graduate programmes.

Businesses are constantly challenged to reinvent their organisations and their leadership systems, and case studies are a way of inducing learning. Case studies as adult learning concepts can help leaders to take up a reflective, inquiring and open attitude toward their own leadership practices.

We recommend that companies provide frameworks for learning in such a fashion that they can then obtain the greatest possible use from the individual learning processes of the students as leaders for organisational learning. This means involvement in the case studies, requests for reports, presentations of the case studies and discussion of these within the company. It is advantageous to establish a mentor relationship between the student and a senior leader of the company which the student works for and which is also the location of the case study. This ensures that the student's work on the case study has the company's backing and facilitates the company's learning from the case study. Post-graduate leadership programmes obtain possibilities for answers to the questions of how in the university sector one can convert from the classic Master's thesis process to the case study process, how a scientific approach to academic papers can link practice and theory, and finally how a form of adult learning can be transferred to academic practice.

We wish you exciting reading!

Maria Spindler
Eva Maria Bauer

Maria Spindler . Martin Steger

The scientific methodology of research case studies

Series editors' foreword

Research "between university and corporation" takes place when it is dedicated on the one hand to pragmatic requirements, economic process logic and product logic and on the other hand to theoretical demands and scientific discourse."[1] These were the opening words of the first volume of our book series "Between University and Organization". The present second volume substantiates this claim by using a particular form of research as example: the research case study or single case study. It is, in our opinion, particularly suited to explore this area of conflict and the possibilities it contains, because it is located at the interface of the logics, which are addressed. The qualitative case studies collected in this volume, however, also unite corporate and university perspectives on a thematic level. They are drawn from Master's theses written to satisfy degree requirements of the postgraduate course of study "Communication and Leadership" at the "Center for Journalism and Communication Management" and are characterized by the fact that the authors deepened and broadened their professional expertise and experience through a scientific approach.

Admittedly the scientific status of such case studies is consistently contested with the argument that their value lies more in the field of didactics and, while they can help their authors to understand their professional areas better, they hardly provide scientifically valid results in the strict sense. The authors would be, as a rule, too involved to be objective, and in principle the methods permit no generalized conclusions, but at most first insights, which then must be corroborated through objective procedures.

In our opinion and experience, this criticism is both too severe and too lenient: it is too severe because it designates one of the risks of this method as a principal reservation. It is in fact a risk of case studies that the researcher will remain too fixated on the specific constellation of the individual case and not be able to work out structural aspects of general significance, just as the risk of quantitative studies is that the researcher will abstract too much

---

1 Spindler, M./Steger M. (2010).

from the complexity of reality to be able to provide relevant results. This is, however, far more a criterion by which one can recognize successful case studies than a fate in store for all of them–unless one requires them to provide results of the same objective-prognostic character as those provided by natural science-oriented qualitative studies. In that case, however, it would be necessary to reach agreement among various areas of cultural and social sciences within the scientific community,[2] since they deal with the interpretation of an ambiguously structured world, not with the description of an unambiguously dutiful world, provided the natural science research paradigm can and wants to uphold this claim.[3] The criticism is, however, also too lenient if it simply politely admits that case studies may not be scientifically valid but nevertheless may help researchers to throw light on their own professional fields.

A successful case study achieves either both or neither because its illuminative potential lies in the scientific approach. A successful research case study offers the possibility of going beyond the purely subjective horizon of experience through identification and clarification of general structural aspects–also called "structural generalizations".

In order to evaluate more precisely what case studies can achieve, it is necessary to recall their research logic: in general one applies the term "research case studies" to scientific studies which select a single element–an event or a delimitable unit (object, person, organization, system) as their object of investigation–and then observe, describe and analyze it. This mainly makes sense when the point is "to draw an integrated and realistic picture of the social world,"[4] which factors in as many relevant dimensions and aspects of the object of investigation as possible. The methodological diversity of case studies is correspondingly broad.[5] In principle, it is not a common methodology which unites case studies, but rather a common research paradigm. In the precise investigation of an example from the real world which was randomly or systematically selected as especially typical or especially distinctive, one can analyze structural conditions which systematically influence the object and actions under investigation. These structural conditions then analogously influence analogous cases, which share the same aspects of the world. Therefore case studies investigate a particular case not only with

---

2 Cf. Habermas, J. (1991, 29).
3 The limits of this claim are also recorded in the scientific theory of the natural sciences, not later than with quantum theory and the constructivist description of circular phenomena. Cf. Foerster, Heinz von (1985).
4 Lamnek, S. (1995, 5).
5 Cf. Bauer, E. M./Ettl-Huber, S. (2012).

the intention of learning about the case itself, but also of working out what is general within the specific; thus they are the prototype of inductive procedure in science.

In this basic characteristic of the inductive approach, the scientific method of case studies is not seriously contested. The inductive knowledge gained from individual observations is principally indispensable, as well as having become virtually de rigeur in science, from its history to its present. From Galileo's observations of Jupiter's moons to Lewin's field studies, from Lazarsfeld's study of the unemployed in Marienthal to Penzia and Wilson's discovery of cosmological radiation. Individual case studies stand at the beginning of almost every innovative process in which new fundamental knowledge was generated. In this principle of structural-analogous generalization of a paradigmatically successful individual case, Thomas Kuhn sees a fundamental principle of further development of science itself.[6]

However, the scientific reputation of case studies also depends to a great extent on their methodological approach and context, and then above all on how they try to ensure the objectivity and generalizability of their data. The scientific standing of two types of case studies is largely undisputed: One is those case studies which are carried out in connection with quantitative-empirical studies, such as pilot studies, accompanying studies or control studies. A division of labor can be observed here: the quantitative studies provide "hard", generalized data–and are therefore willing to take responsibility for the actual scientific aspect–while the qualitative studies are responsible for the interpretation of correlations. On the one hand right at the beginning, through formulation of hypotheses, so that presumably significant connections can be discovered which can then be quantitatively tested, and on the other hand as proof and illustrations for the interpretation of the results–since what the acquired data actually means cannot be determined beyond dispute by quantitative studies with their own repertoire of methods.

The other widely recognized type of case studies, such as qualitative network analysis[7] or Ulrich Oevermann's objective hermeneutics[8], developed a procedure, which is as differentiated and standardized as possible for data collection and intersubjective interpretation. With the standardized procedure, however, the perspective of the case studies changes. The procedure itself becomes the focus; now there are certain types of cases,

---

6 Kuhn, Th. S. (1997).
7 Cf. Spindler, M./Steger M. (2010, 285 ff).
8 Cf. Wernet, A. (2006).

which are investigated for specific results which the particular procedure can obtain.

With research case studies in the stricter sense–and that is what this volume deals with–the case itself remains the focus viewed from as many different angles as possible. The approach is not strictly prescribed, but develops through the characteristics of the case. Accordingly, these studies are characterized by an open approach with combinations of methods and variations, which nevertheless can include quantitative procedures. Based on the progress of the study and due to preliminary results and structural hypotheses, decisions regarding methods will be modified and reached again and again.

Thus, in the end, every case study has its individual methodological procedure. In fact, in this research design traditional scientific quality criteria from the research paradigm of laboratory experiments, such as objectivity (independence of the results from the individual case) or reliability (reproducibility of the process of cognition) are not, in principle, assured. Instead the focus is on validity (appropriateness of the findings with respect to the object), which is to be ensured as far as possible through research principles such as openness and the ability to be communicated, naturalized and interpreted.[9]

This brings us to a comparison which has often enough been outlined, and which has finally declared the question of the scientific methodology of case studies to be a question of faith. As a prototype of qualitative research, case studies claim higher validity. This higher validity cannot, however, raise the findings above the context of the insight process, that is, make them objective and realiable, as much as quantitative studies can. Case studies have a certain right, in this close interweaving with the object of investigation as a complete phenomenon, to be considered objective in another way– that is object related. However, since the essential function of science is to provide us with knowledge, which is always correct, upon which we can always rely independent of the situation, the doubts about the scientific methodology of case studies cannot in fact be removed.

However, we can go one step further and view science overall as a process of cognition, which would shift the picture of this simple comparison. It can be seen that, although foreign to the logic of case studies, the criteria of objectivity and reliability of scientific claims to reliable and generally valid statements are realized, perhaps not in every single study, but overall in case study research. In addition to the criterion of validity, case studies are defi-

---

9 Cf. Lamnek, S. (1995^3, 17 ff).

nitely oriented to the demands of objectivity by working out general structures, which promise orientation values beyond the individual case. Depending on relevance and appropriateness, these structures will be taken up in further studies–yet another reason why, as a rule, case studies clarify to a high degree the state of the art of the level of knowledge concerning the context of the phenomenon under investigation. These structures are not, however, used as indespensible knowledge, independent of context, but as a pattern of analysis, which is subordinated to, compared with, newly contextualized and modified by the specific characteristics of the new case. This way conclusions do not result from the principle of situation-independent findings but from structural analogy and repetitions, which are not identical but varied. These conclusions are increasingly context-free and general and can be confidently treated as reliable and objective.

This contextual freedom, however, is not a lack of context but an independence from various elevated contexts upon which the conclusions can be, but no longer need to be based, and through which in addition the fundamental common structures can be seen in relation to each other. Analogous to the principle of systematic variations of quantitative studies, these conclusions increasingly gain scope as knowledge. Both secure and varied structural insights, which are often picked up also permit findings, which are ever more differentiated and can increasingly do justice to the dynamics and complexity of our everyday life. In this way the results of the previously mentioned study of Marienthal, claiming that the long-term unemployed tend not to become politicized and revolutionary but much more depoliticized and resigned, which were confirmed in many further studies, were decontextualized as general knowledge–in many different contexts: How does this tendency change with social development, with various accompanying circumstances, etc.?

This procedure of generalization and simultaneous differentiation of structural insights from individual case studies is thus found as a methodological procedure in more complex studies such as the work of Pierre Bourdieu and Michel Foucault.[10] They are based on the meta-analysis of case studies and many complex scenarios of descriptions of reality derive from them. In an additional step, a multiplicity of further studies is based on these, so that separate branches of research, such as governmentality research develop. So, instead of dealing with a homogenous canon of knowl-

---

10 In Bourdieu's work on corresponding analytical generalization procedures, in Foucault's work, for example, in the development of the panopticon on structurally analogous generalization procedures.

edge, we in qualitative research have to deal with a complex field of bodies of knowledge, which have been acquired through case studies which refer to each other. Around a central, certain and complex contextualized gist are grouped findings with differing degrees of certainty and variation along a scale between theory and real life. The scientist's expertise consists not only of the mastery of a canon of knowledge and ability, but also of the ability to move routinely in this field of findings of varying degrees of specificity and validity.

This characteristic of qualitatively won knowledge means that the following points are involved when dealing with case studies in general and with every individual case study:

- On the one hand they are complicated, because we do not simply deal with "true statements" upon which we can rely, but rather with proposals for structuring–enriched by specific data–which we can only consider with regard to its own contexts. These proposals can fit another situation but need not. They must first be interpreted for each individual context.
- On the other hand, the very abundance of case studies means that they simultaneously refer both to practical and to theoretical contexts in varying degrees of generality.

Andreas Wernet sees the concept of the case as "a connecting link, a moment of intervention"[11] between theory and practice: "The concept of the case points to that dialectic of the general and the specific which we have become aware of from a hermeneutic perspective, for it is only within a framework of the general that the specific can become noticeable. The noticeable only becomes visible before a background of expectations of normality. Without these expectations of generality it remains insignificant. Naturally, therefore, the question 'What is the case?' is inextricably linked with the question 'What must be done?'. In this respect a case history-oriented concept of the case is genuinely obligated to a practical interest in action and intervention. At the same time it points to the matter of a theoretical justification and systematization of an intervention which is appropriate to the case."[12]

Thus we have returned to the claims we formulated at the beginning: Case studies are especially suitable for linking corporate and university per-

---

11 Wernet, A. (2006, 113).
12 Ibid.

spectives because they relate the logic of action from the practice field of economics, from which our case studies are drawn, and the theoretical logic of justification of university research interests.

A successful case is therefore in a position to illuminate the professional field as well as to generate theoretical knowledge – and only when both professional field and theoretical knowledge achieve the desired outcome the case can succeed, as both develop together. Case studies general theoretical knowledge by working out general structures from concrete occurrences; in return for this they must draw on and continue to work on existing theoretical contexts and knowledge of structures, thus further enriching and developing these theoretical contexts. At the same time, reflectively referencing the practice field for theoretical explanatory patterns illuminates the occurrence in the practice field itself. This is valid for the authors of our case studies, who are primarily researching their own professional fields, as well as for the readers, because they systematically reconstruct concrete examples and standards for finding solutions in their fields of practice. Thus by simultaneously reflecting the structures which have been worked out onto their own professional experience with respect to gains in explanations and orientation, they learn appropriate theoretical patterns of explanation and how to deal with them. We trust that this volume will do exactly that for you.

> "Common to all experts, however, is that they operate on the basis of intimate knowledge of several thousand concrete cases in their areas of expertise. Context-dependent knowledge and experience are at the very heart of expert activity. Such knowledge and expertise also lie at the center of the case study as a research and teaching method or to put it more generally still, as a method of learning. Phenomenological studies of the learning process therefore emphasize the importance of this and similar methods: It is only because of experience with cases that one can at all move from being a beginner to being an expert. If people were exclusively trained in context-independent knowledge and rules, that is, the kind of knowledge that forms the basis of textbooks and computers, they would remain at the beginner's level in the learning process. This is the limitation of analytical rationality: It is inadequate for the best results in the exercise of a profession, as student, researcher, or practitioner."[13]

---

13 Flyvbjerg B. (2006, 219).

Literature

Flyvbjerg B. (2006), Five Misunderstandings about Case-Study Research. *Qualitative Inquiry.* Vol. 12, Number 2.
Foerster, Heinz von (1985), Sicht und Einsicht. Versuche zu einer operativen Erkenntnistheorie. Vieweg, Braunschweig, Wiesbaden.
Habermas, J. (1991), Moralbewusstsein und kommunikatives Handeln. Suhrkamp, Frankfurt am Main.
Kuhn, T. S. (1997), Die Struktur wissenschaftlicher Revolutionen. Suhrkamp, Frankfurt am Main.
Lamnek, S. (1995), Qualitative Sozialforschung. Vol. 2. Beltz, Psychologie Verlags Union, Weinheim.
Spindler, M./Steger M. (2010), Zwischen Universität und Unternehmen. Kultur-, sozial- und wirtschaftsorientierte Forschung im Spannungsfeld von theoretischen Ansprüchen und praktischen Interessen. Verlagshaus Hernals, Wien.
Wernet, A. (2006), Einführung in die Interpretationstechnik der Objektiven Hermeneutik. Qualitative Sozialforschung. Vol. 11, 2nd edition. VS Verlag, Wiesbaden.
Wernet, A. (2006), Hermeneutik – Kasuistik – Fallverstehen. Grundriss der Pädagogik/Erziehungswissenschaft. Vol. 24. Eds.: Helsper, Kade, Lüders, Radtke. Kohlhammer, Stuttgart.

Silvia Ettl-Huber . Eva Maria Bauer . Michael Roither

From Master's thesis to case study – an approach for challenging MBA theses

Since its founding sixteen years ago, the Center for Journalism and Communication Management at the Danube University Krems has been dealing with organization and mass communication in all its facets. Today, fifteen programmes of advanced academic study covering three subject areas – journalism, public relations and management communication – most of which lead to a Master's degree, are successfully offered in five cities. These programmes focus on applied communication research, which in turn has a central influence on teaching.

Covering the three subject areas with appropriate Master's degree programmes, however, led about six years ago to the request for a Master's degree building on the subject, for practice and for professionally oriented programmes. The content of such a degree was quickly determined: a more global, interdisciplinary, comprehensive consideration of the concepts of communication and leadership.

Accordingly, in 2007 the first Master of Business Administration (MBA) with a concentration on Communication and Leadership was taken as a common next step following a number of Master's programmes (Public Relations and Integrated Communication, Communication and Management, Strategic Information Management, Process Management, Quality Management, Knowledge Management, Technical Communication, Library and Information Management[1]). It offered students in these subject-oriented fields the new opportunity to complete a further degree with a focus on communication and leadership.

The curriculum developed was based upon 'Leading through Communication' and was enriched through additional supporting instructional units in areas such as integrated coaching and peer-group learning.[2] The programme was intended to allow students to reflect on their own roles as managers, not only theoretically but also practically. The question of what the master´s thesis should look like remained open until the end. Because the students had already written Master's theses in their previous studies, the

---

1 Donau-Universität Krems (2006), Mitteilungsblatt 2006/Nr. 57, 13/09/2006
2 Bauer (2006). Folder Professional MBA Communication and Leadership.

usefulness of writing another conventional Master's thesis seemed questionable.

At the same time those responsible for developing the programme carried out an informal survey of the experiences of MBA graduates throughout Austria. The resulting picture was alarming. While most of the respondents praised their MBA tutors, many of them also expressed displeasure with their Master's theses without even being asked. The main points of criticism were lack of support combined with unclear objectives of the MBA Master's theses. Even when those responsible for the programme of study gave a student free rein in the selection of subjects and composition of the thesis and the assessment reports were satisfactory, the board of examiners before whom the Master's thesis was defended was often composed of university professors who were astonished by the less scientific quality of the presentation. The question 'How scientific must the Master's thesis of a business administrator be?' also haunted the developers of the new MBA programme.

Comparison with two MBA programmes by other providers showed that they also required Master's theses. The Executive MBA Communication and Leadership at the Technical University of Munich,[3] for example, plans three months for the completion of a Master's thesis. A precise definition or description of the contents of the Master's thesis, however, does not appear on the official website of the programme. The Malik Master of Management Programme[4] mentions a challenging thesis, but neither the length of the thesis nor a brief description of its form is available online.

From their work with students, the developers of the course of study knew that the motivation to deal with a research question from the student's perspective was high. The employer often finances the study costs at the Danube University Krems, and the Master's thesis offers the students the opportunity to provide a return benefit to their company. Those responsible for developing the programme were nevertheless aware of the potential accusation from the board of examiners that the students would simply put their everyday experience down on paper.

The challenge was therefore to give the students the opportunity to work on their own professional experience and still produce scientifically acceptable, perhaps even exploitable theses. The resulting idea was that the MBA in Communication and Leadership should make a virtue of necessity. Working on a case from the student's own professional experience would not only be allowed, but expressly welcomed. Today the programme has developed

---

3 Technical University of Munich (downloaded on 26/04/2012)
4 Malik Management (downloaded on 26/04/2012)

to the point that students must provide a sketch of the case they propose to work on as part of their application to the MBA programme.

It then became necessary to solve the problem of methodology, since as already described, these case studies had in the past consisted of rather vaguely documented assessment reports, often brimming with personal observations and unfounded evaluations. To make the case study respectable and in particular to make the work process reproducible therefore required a great deal of work. Finding a method, teaching material and method of supervision had to be tackled. (See also the chapter *Supervision of students in the case study process.*)

Today the case study is no longer a compulsory scientific exercise adjacent to all the useful experiences such a study provides. It is rather a central learning experience within the MBA programme. Harald Gansfuss, a graduate of the MBA 03, describes the learning effects of his case study: "For me it was extremely informative to see that not everything is as it appears at first glance. You have to reflect on many things from different perspectives, and ideally many times, in order to get a complete view. It was a learning experience that has remained with me ever since and that I think about often."[5]

Because the case is chosen from the student's own practice, one can see a high degree of student motivation right from the start. This personal involvement combined with the necessary scientific distance leads in the end to an enriched learning experience, since on the one hand the problem at the root of the case study is formulated and the results and circumstances of the case are newly evaluated, while on the other hand a professional distance to cases which are often highly emotional is required. As if in a time machine, students experience their case once again in retrospective with insights which not only relate to the case but also allow them to newly evaluate their own reasoning powers.

Having said that, these case studies often provide interesting contributions to the body of science. (See also the chapter *Case studies: definition, application, strengths.*) On the one hand, data, which are not available to science, are gathered by the authors of the case studies, who are often people with over ten years of professional experience. They often hold leadership positions and can gain access to information, which an external researcher would never get hold of. On the other hand, the methodological development at the interface between theory and practice broadens the spectrum of the scientific work.

In the meantime, experience has been gained from four years and four classes of students in the Communication and Leadership MBA programme,

---

5 Gansfuss (2011), Interview

a time frame, which was absolutely necessary for the presentation of first results. The positive results of the case study Master's theses are certainly not only the result of the case study as such but also of the supervision process, which likewise has been developed around four years of Master's theses. (See also the chapter *Supervision of students in the case study process.*) Notwithstanding, both those responsible for the programme and its graduates are convinced that they have found an approach, which does justice to the requirements of science in a practice-oriented Master's thesis – and thus have developed a first-class MBA programme.

References

Bauer, E. M. (2006), Folder Professional MBA Communication and Leadership. Material is owned by Danube University Krems and not open to public access.
Donau-Universität Krems (2006), Mitteilungsblatt 2006/Nr. 57, 13/09/2006.
http://www.donau-uni.ac.at/imperia/md/content/donau-uni/mitteilungsblaetter/2006/duk_mb_5706.pdf
Gansfuss, H. (2011), Interview with Eva Maria Bauer, 17/08/2011.
Technical University of Munich. Executive MBA in Communication and Leadership. www.communicate-program.de, downloaded on 26/04/2012.
Malik Management. Malik Master of Management® Programme. www.malik-management.com, downloaded on 26/04/2012.

Eva Maria Bauer . Silvia Ettl-Huber

Case studies: definition, application, strengths

1 What is a case study?

In German-language literature on the subject of methods of empirical social research one can read that case studies are not an independent method, but rather serve a complementary function[1]. Lamnek[2] describes case studies as a bundling of methods such as participant observation, interviews, group discussion methods or content analysis of autobiographies, documents, reports and letters. In this context, quantitative research logic prefers techniques such as standardized interviews or observations, while the qualitative paradigm attaches special importance to open and naturalistic-communicative procedures such as group discussions, narrative interviews or participant observation.

So far, so good. But what if it is not methods of collecting and analysing data, which are at the center of the methodological approach but rather the thoughtful application of one or more cases as the starting point for research? What if it is the research attitude of a person involved as a practitioner in a case and who becomes a researcher, which is treated as a decisive methodological asset? Then the case study is no longer a bundle of methods but an independent methodological procedure. We use this approach here as we deal with the definition, application, strengths and weaknesses of the case study.

Case studies target a precise description or reconstruction of a case. The concept of a 'case' is broad – in addition to people, social communities (e.g. families), organisations and institutions (e.g. a residential care home) may be the object of a case analysis[3]. Merriam defines a case study as "an in-depth description and analysis of a bounded system"[4]. Yin defines a case study in terms of the research process: "A case study is an empirical inquiry that investigates a contemporary phenomenon within its real-life context, especial-

---

1 See for example Flick (2009) p. 25.
2 Lamnek (2005) p. 301.
3 Flick (2009) p. 254.
4 Merriam (2009) p. 40.

ly when the boundaries between phenomenon and context are not clearly evident"[5].

As phenomenon and context are not always distinguishable Yin provides a supplementary definition based on technical characteristics. According to this, a case study inquiry is identified in that it

- "copes with the technically distinctive situation in which there will be many more variables of interest than data points, and as one result
- relies on multiple sources of evidence, with data needing to converge in a triangulating fashion and as another result
- benefits from prior development of theoretical propositions to guide data collection and analysis."[6]

Stake[7] emphasizes that the case is an arena to bring many functions and relationships together for study. The selected case (the subject of the case study) is that which is focused on from beginning to end of the investigation. The case study is thus neither an exclusively qualitative nor an exclusively quantitative method, or as Stake makes clear with this illustration: "[...] the physician's record of the [ill] child is more quantitative than qualitative. The social worker studies the child because the child is neglected. [...] The formal record that the social worker keeps is more qualitative than quantitative."[8] In this context Merriam[9] also stresses the importance of historical data.

The primary authority for data collection and analysis thereby is the researcher. Merriam emphasizes the need for an inner connection between the researcher and the phenomenon to be observed. She writes: "If the phenomenon is not intrinsically bounded, it is not a case"[10]. In this context she explains two ways to uncover this boundedness. One technique for assessing the boundedness of the topic is to ask how finite the data collection would be, that is, whether there is a limit to the number of people involved who could be interviewed or whether there is a finite time for observations.[11]

She further mentions that a bounded system, or case, might be selected because it is an instance of some process, issue, or concern. If the researcher

---

5   Yin (2008) p.13.
6   Yin (2008) pp. 13–14.
7   Stake (2006) p. 2.
8   Stake (2005) p. 443.
9   Merriam (2009) p. 39.
10 Merriam (2009) p. 41.
11 Merriam (2009) pp. 41 f.

is interested in the process of changing the organisational culture of the workplace, for example, he or she could select a particular instance of organisational change to study in-depth.[12]

In contrast to case studies involving a personal connection, Stake[13] lists three approaches to case studies, based upon determining whether the researcher approaches the case with an intrinsic or an instrumental interest: the resulting three types are intrinsic case study, instrumental case study and multiple case study, also called collective case study. He refers to an intrinsic case study when the primary reason for undertaking the case study is to obtain a better understanding of a particular case. Instrumental case studies, on the other hand, study a particular case in order to derive generalisations. Multiple case studies also look at generalisations but also at a number of cases. Interest in individual cases is not the primary focus and, further, interest in the cases will be primarily instrumental.

The focus in this journal is on single cases. To a great extent this relates to the specific situation of the students, who are working full-time; they nearly all (want to) choose to work with a case from their relevant professional experience. It also relates to the fact that the length of a Master's thesis is better suited to the study of a single case than of multiple cases.

2 The difference between research case studies and teaching cases

Merriam's[14] historical view shows that the term "case study" had already appeared as a method in literature of the 1960s, mostly as a variation of experimental designs and statistical methods.

"Some of the texts of the 1960s included a final chapter named 'Case Studies' wherein it was acknowledged that there existed the occasional historical or in-depth descriptive study of a phenomenon"[15].

In the 1980s authors like Yin (1984), Stake (1988), and Merriam herself (1988) dealt explicitly with the case study as a method. Since then the method has been constantly further developed, and the fundamental research has been published in numerous revised editions.

---

12   Merriam (2009) pp. 41 f.
13   Stake (2006) p. 8.
14   Merriam (2009) p. 39.
15   Merriam (2009) p. 39 f.

Merriam describes it thus: "[...] part of the confusion surrounding case studies is [...] the process of conducting a case study is conflated with both the unit of study (case) and the product of this type of investigation."[16]

Closely related to this confusion is the confusion of so-called research case studies in comparison to teaching cases. Teaching case studies are used in various disciplines such as law, business or medicine for a better understanding of working situations. According to Garvin[17], the case study method (here "teaching case method") first appeared in 1870 in the education of students of law at the Harvard Graduate School of Business Administration. A newly appointed dean collected a representative set of court decisions and used them to compile the first legal casebook. He used a question-and-answer format in order to be sure that the students learned adequately from the cases.

For teaching purposes, a case study need not contain a complete or accurate rendition of actual events. According to Yin[18] the purpose of a teaching case is to encourage debate among students. What makes a good teaching case is primarily determined by whether the central message is well expressed through the case. The criteria for developing good cases for teaching are different from those for doing a research case study. While pedagogical considerations are the main focus of teaching case studies and scientific accuracy must occasionally be sacrificed, research case studies focus on the rigorous scientific presentation of empirical data.

The discussion of the boundaries between research study and teaching case is not made easier by the existence of mixed forms of case studies which demand scientific accuracy and which postulate, but which on the other hand in their implementation speak of uncertainty and of the students' options for interpretation[19].

3 Application of research case studies

The question which research procedures the case study is appropriate for cannot be answered with a formula, but Yin provides the following guidance for the decision: "The more your questions seek to explain some present circumstance (e.g. 'how' or 'why' some social phenomenon works), the

---

16   Merriam (2009) p. 40.
17   Garvin (2003) p. 56.
18   Yin (2009) p. 5.
19   Ellet (2008), pp. 24 f.

more the case study method will be relevant."[20] The case study becomes even more interesting as an instructional method when an in-depth description of a social phenomenon has an important place in it and/or when it presents a topical question, which is occasionally difficult to research, over which the researcher has little or no control.[21]

Sylvie Chetty also emphasizes the appropriacy of the case study for 'how' and 'why' questions. Among other questions, she researched how and why firm competencies are related to export performance. From what she learned in this case study of small and medium-sized firms, six key features of case studies can be derived:

1. "The case study method of research is a rigorous methodology that allows decision-making processes and causality to be studied. It is suitable when 'how' and 'why' questions are asked about a set of events. For example, how are firm competencies related to export performance and why are they related?
2. The case study method allows the researcher to study a topic, for example, exporting as a dynamic process, not as something static.
3. The case study method is ideal for studying research topics where existing theory is inadequate.
4. The case study method allows the firm to study from multiple perspectives rather than the influence of a single variable.
5. Multiple-data collection methods allow a more thorough examination of each firm than a narrowly-defined quantitative study. This enables the researcher to become deeply knowledgeable about each firm thus allowing new insights about the topic to emerge.
6. Cross-industry biases, small size of sample, and resistance to survey methods – all these problems are avoided."[22]

4 Strengths of the research case study

Yin[23] describes research case studies as instructional methods, which are meant to contribute to our knowledge of individual, group, organizational, social, political and related phenomena in many different disciplines such

---

20   Yin (2009) p. 4.
21   Yin (2009) p. 13.
22   Chetty (1996) p. 82.
23   Yin (2009) p. 3.

as psychology, social work, political science, anthropology, business, education, nursing and community planning. Case studies are even found in economics, in which the structure of a given industry or economy of a city or region are investigated. The strength of case studies lies in their ability to make complex social phenomena comprehensible. The German researcher of methods, Atteslander[24], stresses their ability to provide detailed findings on social processes.

Generally, case studies are acknowledged to have the ability to reflect holistic images of real-life situations and results. A further strength is that they use many sources of information, not limiting themselves to the method of data collection and analysis.

Merriam[25] characterizes case studies as particularistic, descriptive, and heuristic:

Particularistic means that case studies focus on a particular situation, event, program, or phenomenon. This focus makes case studies especially interesting for practical problems occurring in everyday practice. The case itself is important for what it reveals about the phenomenon.

Descriptive means that at the end of a case study there is a rich description of the phenomenon under study. Merriam uses the expression "thick description"[26], a term from anthropology, to mean the complete, literal description of the incident or entity being investigated. Cases studies contain as many variables as possible and portray their interaction, often over a longer period of time.

Heuristic means that the case study helps the reader to understand the phenomenon under study. They can reveal something new, expand the reader's experience, or confirm what he already knows.

From the supervision experience of the MBA program 'Communication and Leadership', which includes the writing of a Master's thesis (See also the chapter: Supervision of the students in the case study process), the student's learning experience as a researcher can also be emphasized as an asset of the case study. Through the scientific analysis of cases, which have a more or less direct effect on the researcher, he achieves completely new perspectives outside his personal area of concern. In turn, the interplay between scientific distance and a personal approach enriches the research case study and the scientific result.

---

24 Atteslander (2010) p. 61.
25 Merriam (2009) pp. 43–44.
26 Merriam (2009) pp. 43–44.

5 Challenges for the research case study

Despite this positive appraisal of the strengths of case studies, there remains the criticism of the method. A primary point of criticism derives from the quality of many existing case studies. Yin[27] takes up the accusation that too many times case study investigators have been sloppy and unsystematic or have allowed equivocal evidence or biased views to influence the direction of the findings and conclusions. Such lack of scientific honesty is less likely to be present when using other methods – possibly because of the existence of numerous methodological texts providing investigators with specific procedures to be followed. He furthermore mentions that people confuse case study teaching with case study research (see above). The potential for confusion between research case studies and storytelling projects[28] should also be mentioned.

Experience from the supervision of the case studies from which excerpts are presented here (See also the chapter: Supervision of the students in the case study process) also shows that the introduction to the methodical procedure is a constant challenge in the supervision process, all the more because it is nearly always the case that multiple methods of data collection and analysis are used. One situation, which is a particular challenge for research practitioners, is that dealing with scientific methods is not an everyday occurrence for them. While this supervision is of a more technical nature, support for the maintenance of a research perspective extends into the field of psychology. Sometimes in the retrospective description of a case, emotional memories are awakened which can significantly hinder the research perspective.

From the point of view of scientific recognition of the results of case studies, a further point of criticism is the lack of scientific generalisation from case studies. Atteslander[29], for example, in describing the disadvantages of the case study, points out that no statistical representativity is given and that the findings are difficult to communicate. One point of this controversy is discussed (See also the chapter: What leaders can learn through the case study process). Although — as mentioned above — Stake, in his definition of three types of case study, operates on the assumption that the choice may very well be made between a number of cases or the conscious choice of one case with an eye to a desired generalisation; nevertheless, in everyday scien-

---

27 Yin (2009) p. 14.
28 Merriam (2009) pp. 202 f.
29 Atteslander (2010), p. 61.

tific practice, generalisations from a single case are rare. They are usually based on a set of multiple experiments that replicated the same phenomenon under different conditions[30]. Yin[31] however points out that case studies, like experiments, are generalizable to theoretical propositions and not to populations or universes. In this sense, the case study, like the experiment, does not represent a sample. In doing a case study, the goal will be to expand and generalize theories (analytical generalization) and not to enumerate frequencies (statistical generalization).

Gary[32] works out the difference between case study, survey and experiment. In contrast to survey and experiment, a case study investigates only one or a few cases, but in return collects comparatively much material for investigation. Other than experiment and survey, quantification in case studies is not a priority, but rather many methods and sources of data are used. The case study pursues the goal of investigating relationships and processes, while the experiment looks at causation and the survey looks for generalization. In comparing case study and experiment, Merriam[33] also stresses that one strength of an experimental design, for example, is the predictive nature of research findings. Because of the highly controlled conditions, random sampling, and use of statistical probabilities, it is theoretically possible to predict behaviour in similar settings without actually observing that behaviour. If the researcher needs information about the characteristics of a given population of area or interest, a descriptive study is needed.

A further point of criticism of case studies, which Yin[34] worked out, is that case studies often drown in material or present their findings in thick, unreadable documents. Yin rebuts this accusation by saying that the practice of the presentation of case studies is constantly being further developed.

The case studies included in this reader are presented as examples within a strictly formal framework. They may not exceed a maximum length of seventy to eighty pages. Thirty to forty pages are intended for the presentation of the case, and fifteen to twenty pages for the theory. Included within the total page count are abstract, introduction, transitions, case, theory and concluding summary. Alongside the practical consideration of keeping the supervision manageable are the considerations that the length of the pres-

---

30 Yin (2009) p. 14.
31 Yin (2009) p. 14.
32 Gary (2011) pp. 10 f.
33 Merriam (2000) pp. 50 f.
34 Yin (2009) p. 15.

entation of the material in each case is gradable and that conciseness is more important than amplitude.

The experience gained through the MBA program presented here showed another weakness of case studies. In the early years of the program, students almost always refused to allow public access to their case studies. Because sensitive data and deep insights into individual organizations were presented, they did not want their findings made available to the public. This problem still exists; however, students now receive intensified guidance on making their cases more anonymous, which also benefits the scientifically distanced mindset of the researchers.

In summary, for this definition and application of case studies it must be stressed that case studies are not considered here as a bundling of methods but as a completely independent method. The justification for this lies in the role of the researcher, who makes an essential contribution through the selection of the case and his approach to it. Thus at the end of the day the case is not only the common denominator on the shoulders of which methods can be bundled, but also the starting point and success factor for the research result.

In the process it is important to differentiate between research case study and teaching case study. The teaching case study serves teaching purposes. For this reason it is important that the material to be taught is ideally presented in the case. Scientific accuracy is not the priority. There are in fact elements of storytelling included in a teaching case, with the goal of anchoring knowledge from the case in the minds of the learners through stories. Research case studies, on the other hand, seek to work on and answer research questions. Precision in application of scientific methods and confirmability of scientific procedure are the focus. A (partial) failure in the handling of the question is also possible. No statements, which are not scientifically tenable, are 'forced' in order to follow teaching goals. A great strength of the research case study in comparison with other methods is described as its ability to deal with 'why' and 'how' questions, to deal with questions, which are (even more) difficult to research, and to combine scientific methods of data collection and analysis. This combination of methods in practice, however, yields a point of criticism if in the execution every method is not well used. Through the bundling of methods within the case study, every criticism of the individual methods (e.g. the content analysis) affects the case study as a whole.

In this sense the case study, observed in its individual parts, is criticisable, but in comparison in its focus on only one or a few cases it is powerful because it centers the question again and again on one single case. Discrepancies in the particular results can thus in the consolidation of results be recognized in the case, and the depth of the insights can be increased through the immersion in the case.

References

Atteslander, Peter (2010), Methoden der empirischen Sozialforschung. 13th edition, Erich Schmidt, Berlin.
Chetty, Sylvie (1996), The Case Study Method for Research in Small and Medium-sized Firms. In: *International Small business journal* 1996, 15/1, p. 73–84.
Flick, Uwe/von Kardoff, Ernst/Steinke, Ines (2009), Was ist qualitative Forschung? In: Flick, Uwe/von Kardoff, Ernst/Steinke, Ines: Qualitative Forschung. Ein Handbuch. 7th edition (p. 25–26). rowohlts enzyklopädie, Reinbek bei Hamburg.
Garvin, David A. (2003), Making the Case. Professional education for the world of practice. In: *Harvard Magazine*, September-October 2003, 106/1, p. 56–107.
Gary, Thomas (2011), How to do Your Case Study. Guide for Students & Researchers. Sage, Los Angeles, London, New Delhi, Singapore, Washington DC.
Lamnek, Siegfried (2005), Qualitative Sozialforschung. Lehrbuch. 4th edition, Beltz, Basel.
Merriam, Sharan B. (2009), Qualitative Research. A Guide to Design and Implementation. Jossey-Bass, San Francisco.
Stake, Robert E. (2005), Qualitative Case Studies. In: Denzin, Norman K./Lincoln Yvonna S. (Eds.): The Sage Handbook of Qualitative Research. 3rd edition, (p. 443–466). Sage, Thousand Oaks, London, New Delhi.
Stake, Robert E. (2006), Multiple Case Study Analysis. The Guilford Press, New York.
Yin, Robert K. (2009), Case Study Research. Design and Methods. 4th edition. Sage, Thousand Oaks, London, New Delhi.

Maria Spindler

Organizations and their Interplay with Leadership for an Uncertain Future
Seven Principles

On the one hand the future is uncertain, complex and therefore unpredictable. On the other hand leaders can and should influence the future. Dealing with different perspectives and creating a future together is essential for leadership in order to reach a position from which it can truly grasp the environment and the future of the organization[1]. This requires of leadership a reflective perception of itself as a system having to deal with the uncertainty of the outcome of leadership actions and of the future.

Leadership is viewed here as bearing responsibility for an organization as a complete system[2], internally and externally. For the organization this means an investment in leadership learning, which calls for the development of an internal capability. A conscious decision for an investment in leadeårship capacity as well as in a unique identity is helpful. Providing orientation for the development of this leadership capacity is the goal of this article. The following principles are to be understood as conditions and opportunities for leadership, so that consciousness and responsibility may be established for the development of functional and socially sustainable organized communication[3].

---

1 An organization is viewed here as a social conception, as organised communication.
2 Also understood as general management. Wimmer/Schumacher (2009, p. 176 ff) speak of general management, which assumes responsibility for caring for the complete organization and with it the task of organization and leadership. They discuss in detail the responsibilities of general management for the complete system and speak of six central areas of leadership responsibility: organization, resources, markets and environment, the future, the present, and people.
3 This observation is based on complex relationships, which is why the focus is on the form of organized communication as a leadership task, especially on requirements and opportunities. When trying to understand complex phenomena such as organization and leadership in terms of communication, it is an advantage to have a definition of communication which can provide an organizational complexity in line with global complexity–and which can, according to Baecker, serve as a basic definition for communication. Based on a first distinction, a highly differentiated

Principle 1: Leadership action is based on observation

In modern communication and organization sciences communication is understood as that which unites the parts. Defining communication as a 'third entity' brings the whole and the relationship of its parts to each other into focus. Communication becomes the object of observation: communication between organization and society, between leadership systems and organizations, between employees, between teams, between organizations and their markets, etc. "If we want to know how communication works, we have to learn to observe[4] not only the participants and parts but also a third entity, the opening and closing of room to maneuver."[5] In this way, more communicative complexity in the relationship of the parts to each other can be comprehended. Communication is not assigned to the individual actors ("He or she communicates well.") but communication (and of course organized communication, organization and leadership as well) is observed as an object, a third entity. ("The organization as system communicates.")

Organised communication can be observed in different degrees of complexity.[6] A very low level of complexity would be a 'technical' approach such as cause and effect. These are relations like 'sender -receiver' or 'input – output'[7]. The relation is perceived and treated in a technical-mechanical way

---

system can be constructed. The complete space, condition or content is designated as a form. See further Spencer-Brown 1969, Baecker 2005, 2007a and Simon 2006.

4 The system theory designation for this is: 1. Observation 2. Organization 3. Observation 4. Organization. With every organization, new differences and thus new borders to the system come into view.

5 Baecker (2007, p. 9)

6 In this context, complexity means the relationship of the individual parts to the whole: the more complexity there is in the way the group in its mutual development can be constructed and handled, the more learning can be generated for complex management situations. The more complex the management situations are, the less the management requirements can be explained simply by the characteristics and actions of the individual parts. System theory takes up the cybernetic representation of complex dynamic phenomena and, with the functional analysis of social, sense-limited, complex dynamic systems (and organizations are counted among these), can conceive of complexity in new ways. The actor moves to the background, together with his intentions. With Kant's concept of the human as a rational being, ideas both of the world and of the ways in which humans deal with it become continuously more complex. See further the comprehensive discussion in Spindler, M. / Steger, M. (2008, 237 ff).

7 See further Baecker (2005), Morgan (2006), Förster, H. von (1985 and 1988), Spinder/Steger (2008).

that can be useful in perceiving technical communication systems as we use them for hierarchical structures. In leadership terms this correlates with the hierarchical[8] approach of 'command - fulfilment'. The leader observes him/herself as directly influencing the organization or the parts of the organization for which he is responsible. Due to its concreteness, low level of complexity and rigidity, this image of organization and leadership is easy to comprehend. What leadership observes and interprets on an organizational level can be planned and changed on the organizational level.

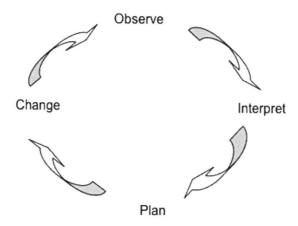

Figure 1: Action Circle – according to Lewin[9]

It would be dysfunctional if organizational phenomena that are essential for survival were not perceptible to leadership, since they are designed multidimensionally rather than linearly. That these simple, technical-linear work processes have been and continue to be taken over more and more by machines is no coincidence.

Complex organizational activities such as market cultivation, tailor-made products, client orientation, internationalization, knowledge work and mind work[10] require complex cognitive capabilities. This goes hand-in-hand with

---

8   Gerhard Schwarz (2007) describes the hierarchy as "die Heilige Ordnung der Männer" (English: the holy order of men).
9   See further Lewin (1946).
10 See inter alia Willke 2007. He speaks of a knowledge society when qualitative new forms of the basis of knowledge and symbolization of all important areas of a society pervade that society. The functional systems of the society (politics, economy, science, etc.) cannot stand for the whole without deforming the complete society. He also points out that, even in a knowledge society, not all communication is affected by knowledge criteria.

the flexibility of organizations: a low degree of complexity is perfect for situations where the communication pattern is exactly the same all the time, where there is only one possible way to respond and where the counterpart acts mechanically, like a machine.[11] It shows the logic of hierarchical communication patterns. Where functionality (utility) is concerned, this form is optimal for recurring tasks. For example, assembly line work is structured so that machine-like behavior is required of humans; the decision for this procedure is delegated upwards.

Principle 2: Communitized observation is the leverage for complex leadership actions

The capacity for observation as leadership system is a central requirement for the complex-functional perception and the possibilities for interpretation and action of organized communication, which build upon it. This is consistent with the external demands on organizations in the uncertain future of the 'next society.'[12]

Communitized observation as leadership system unites the perspective of the individual leaders with those of the organization. The leadership system is able to observe, interpret, plan and finally act or change reflectively on a bigger scale with more diversity. Communitized observation of an organization is created with the differences, which this entity (the organization) contains. Through the shared effort of observation, a picture of the organization as a communicative entity of action is created – it is to be understood as a communitized abstraction.

With the concept of the communitized abstraction[13], the requirement of having <u>one</u> truth is relinquished. Everyone can observe, recognize and inter-

---

11 The distinction between trivial and non-trivial machines was introduced by Heinz von Foerster (1985). The trivialization of a system consists in reducing it to the model machine. The trivial machine is a machine that repeats without error. Trivial machines are often formal means of grasping living complex systems. The non-trivial machine is a machine, which is so complex as to prevent an analytical knowledge of its operation.

12 Baecker places the transition from 'modern society' to 'next society' against a background of observations from cultural and communication theory, especially the effects of computers on our social order. (Baecker 2007b)

13 Since Immanuel Kant, the observation perspective has been seen as a central starting point for science and scientific awareness. In "system theory" we speak of observation as 1. Organization. 2. Organization. 3. Organization.

pret various facts and truths about the organization. There is no one single truth in this collaborative process; participants observe and interpret mutually and equally in order to take the step to the organizational level of an attitude of multiple perspectives of observation and interpretations. This shared process requires that the participants learn how to exchange different truths (a dialog), especially when these truths are in conflict.

Thus communitized abstraction creates a distance from one's own leadership actions, and critical questioning towards the system as whole becomes possible[14].

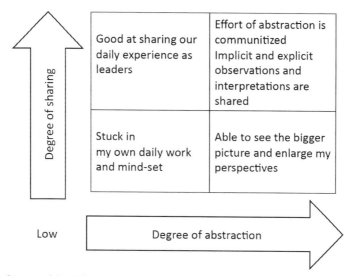

Figure 2: Communitized abstraction

This enrichment as a leadership system forms a culture of acting and observing as an entity and thus enables getting a bigger picture of the environment. Questioning of internal decisions, structures, leadership concepts, processes is supported, as well as forms of cooperation in their interrelations, and changing and developing them appropriately in response to external and future identity requirements. Functional, self-responsible decisions can then be placed at the center and:

- approaching the inter-independent relationship of the organization to the environment (society, market) from a new perspective;

---

14 This concept refers to Peter Senge's "system thinking" (2006), Luhmann's "the system as one unit and its parts with their differences" (2006) and Scharmer's "ecosystem as the system for innovation" (2009).

- providing freedom from sacred traditions;
- focusing usefulness as defined by goals and/or strategy;
- broadening or limiting possibilities for action through decisions and structure[15];
- providing shared learning through "leadership errors" without assigning blame, enabling mutual learning in terms of the development of the complete system[16].

Developing a leader´s capacity for matering uncertainties requires collaborative abstraction as a central condition for the creation of a multi-functional, diverse and contractive perception.

Collaborative abstraction is to be understood here as the idea that leadership can make both itself and the organization (with all of its parts and environments) the object of analysis, evaluation and learning and can selectively design these. Complex and functional leadership:

- asks the question of usefulness in terms of focusing on the goal,
- can either expand or limit options through decisions and structure,
- provides freedom from patterns which have grown sacred over time,
- can learn from management errors without immediately assigning blame to people, thus enabling mutual research and communitized learning with regard to the development of the complete system and its boundaries in its environment,
- can use the diversity of the environment as possibilities by building internal multi-perspectivity and diversity.

Principle 3: Complex organizations as self-responsible entities within an uncertain environment

All external points of reference used by an organization are as a result treated as internal decisions. A decision is what the organization internally regards as a decision. However, internal authority can become dependent on where it supposes the best access to resources for its own survival (clients, contracting entities, political instances, etc.). This "unsettled, complex en-

---

15 Baecker (2007a) speaks of form and forms of communication.
16 Empirical case studies have shown that there can only be learning on an organizational level if the culture of the (individual) blame and exclusion can be overcome. See Spindler (2010).

vironment" is simultaneously an opportunity and a danger, depending on how the organization is able to encounter it. Self-attribution of decisions by leadership is pivotal for their own perception of self-determination and identity building, and for taking responsibility for a complex functional perspective of the organization.

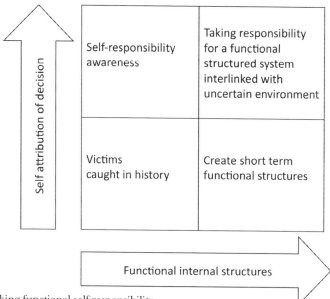

Figure 3: Taking functional self-responsibility

A focus in long-term considered organizations is on the leadership's awareness of the decisive demarcation, meaning decision-making as self-attribution. There is no external power; there is noone to blame. We as a system decide and we are responsible for coping with external and internal opportunities for the organization. We are not victims; we have an active role and we are responsible for what we focus on and what we decide.

Principle 4: Organization seen as self-responsible units and their relation with their environment

Concepts like 'system theory'[17] and 'system thinking'[18] define an organization as a decision-making entity. They recreate and define themselves again

---

17 Cf. Luhmann (1986).
18 Cf. Senge (2006).

and again. This constant self-reflection enables building up identity and sense-making.[19] System-concepts can be applied to individuals, teams, departments, organizations and society[20]. Systems are on the one hand self-steering on the other dependent on their environment[21]. They have the potential to choose their dependence consciously – they are inter-independent. Questioning relationships of dependence and dealing with expectations, contradictions and dilemmas between inter-independent sense-making entities (society, company, sub-systems, employees as a system, the individual as a system) create potential to act more consciously.

Organizations[22] come into being and sustain themselves through differentiation of their environment. Demarcation between an organization and its environment is meaningful when the organization sees itself as complex. The decision[23] for self-attribution generates borders with the environment and leaves that for or against which the organization did not actively decide outside, in the environment. All parts and differences that find their way into the process of linking a decision with another decision belong to the organization's system; all others are seen as environment. One can also say that the decision to differentiate and the internal linking of decisions bring the organization to life and keep it alive.

The relation between organization and environment as vibrating boundaries is not fixed but functionally created with each decision-making. I call it "vibrating" to emphasise the action and change wich is made with each decision. The internal awareness and decision to draw boundaries between the organization and its environment is a continuous and living process in perspectives appropriate to the requirements (functionality); this decision is

---

19 This concept parallels Schein in the way he describes structures as cultural patterns of organizations.
20 Cf. Schneider (1987).
21 The former Eastern European countries can be seen as study subjects from central-organised to complex-organised market structures. See Puffer/McCarthy (2011).
22 Cf. in this context the extensive discussion by Luhmann (2006). He developed a theory of the organization as a social system. He saw organizations not as content-relatedly rational earmarked categories, which orient themselves toward goals, like organizations which are for-profit entities, but rather from the aspect of survival and adaptability. Luhmann sees organizations functionally, based on the principle of survivability (adaptability).
23 Here "decision" in relation to organizations does not mean a mental process or a conscious determination. A decision as an element of the organization is a social event and is thus communication. It arises and disappears immediately at the moment it comes into being. Since a decision is not capable of continued existence it cannot be changed, but it will provoke subsequent decisions.

Social sustainability dimension 1:
The relation between organization and environment as vibrating boundaries

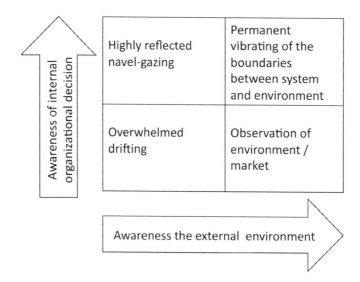

Figure 4: Vibrating of boundaries between system and environment

the occasion for self-responsibility and self-direction. Actively shaping the uncertain environment through reduction by decision-making and structural formation is essential for survival of organizations within an uncertain environment. This is a leadership style with which the organization builds independence from its environment by internally structuring the communication. The leadership and organization bear their own responsibility, thus providing a basis for developing a unique identity for the organization.

Principle 5: Questioning, scrutinizing and future-oriented functionality

Leadership has to counter external societal complexity with internal organized complexity. To do this, it has to develop a sense-making functionality instead of a sacred order[24]. This theoretical concept of organised communi-

---

24 Schwarz (2007) discusses the holy order of men, which is not questionable. Ashkenas, Ulrich, Jick, Kerr (1992) refer to the boundaryless organization, which means

cation systems leads to a perspective that sees organisations no longer as static organisational forms where the existing organization and leadership concept remain unquestioned: an ineffective leadership culture is taken as given. Structures, processes, cultures and leadership concepts have to be questioned. Dynamic organisations require organisational learning, which expects leadership to develop structures and leadership tailored to meet requirements from the environment and internal diversity needs, and to constantly scrutinize them. The hierarchical organisation form is "given by God". In order to get an idea of the complexity of the organizational abstraction with respect to balancing oneness with structural and cultural differences, it is necessary to work with the idea that leadership intervention must move away from unquestioned thought patterns. Active forming of the future presupposes an attitude of questioning.[25]

A future-oriented, functional-operational organizational system scrutinizes structural, leadership and cultural patterns and questions on an abstract level: Which structure, which kind of leadership, which culture will get us as a whole organisation (including our environment) moving toward our future? Reference to a meta-level and the common whole in all its variety is vital for this.

Functionality leads to increased cooperation in diverse communication structures.[26] The practice of consulting shows that this diversity brings about confusion, lack of comprehension and conflicts within organizations. Parts are pitted against each other, and the big picture is lost; thereby the future of the whole with its differences is also lost out of sight. Companies usually exhibit various types of patterns and structures[27] in parallel with and superimposed on each other. For example, an organization might:

---

destroying the holy, God-given order: they call it breaking the restricting chains of organizational structure.

25 In addition, see the incisive contribution of Marshall, S./Vaiman, V./Napier, N./Taylor, S./Häselberger, A./Andersen, T. (2010) The End of a 'Period': Sustainability and the Question Attitude.
26 See further Spindler/Steger 2008.
27 Different types of organizations structured according to their decision-making are listed here in progressive order from inflexible complexity reducing to flexible types. Naturally they are all functional for certain purposes:
- Hierarchical structures: Opportunities and uncertainty can be greatly reduced through hierarchical decision-making patterns.
- Matrix structures lose a central reference point but gain in putting different interests (center – market) on an equal footing.
- Heterarchical structures: the multi-poled expert-based units, group-wide functional centers of competence.

- exhibit a matrix structure to support the international connection of clients on various continents, and
- commission projects which span parts of this matrix for development and implementation of innovation, and
- appoint teams which decide on a heterarchical structure, and
- have a production and warehousing system that is primarily hierarchically structured, and
- co-operate as needed in a networking style within a supply chain, among experts, with clients to develop ideas for innovation, etc.

Social sustainability dimension 3: Future-oriented functional abstraction

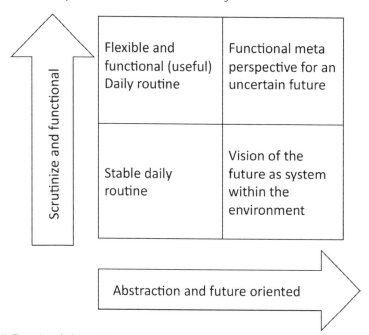

Figure 5: Functional abstraction

- Project structures: assembled for a set period of time in order to accomplish a concrete task. Functionality in decision-making is essential to reach goals.
- Network structures: competence units that are connected with each other through win-win relationships, voluntary participation and trust.

Principle 6: Organizations seen as self-steering transformers of societal complexity

Seeing organizations as transformers of opportunities (complexity), differences and conflicts through decisions gives leadership leverage to decide what should be transformed through the organization. With increasing social complexity, organizations[28] as absorbers and producers of social uncertainty are becoming more and more the center of observation.[29] They are the notable drivers of – and are driven by – dynamics such as globalization, financial crises, questions of human rights and the environment, the knowledge society[30] and computer technologies.

Do we want to reduce our ecological footprint or please our shareholders, or do we want both? The values and identities that come to the fore are the decisions about what we want to transform through our organization. Before a decision is made, there are multiple opportunities; after the decision these opportunities exist as fixed forms. Every decision creates a transformation of opportunities. By making decisions and thus transforming opportunities, an organization manages again and again both to recreate itself and to create opportunities and the necessity for the next decision. By making decisions, organizations reduce the opportunities of the environment and transform them into something new.[31] For this reason organizations also have great influence on both society and individuals.[32]

Against the backdrop of these theoretical considerations, organizations have great potential to operate as transformers of society. It stands to reason that there are links between system theory approaches, which place at the center decisions and structuring that are self-referential and based on per-

---

28 See examples of sustainability display interconnections in Haugh/Talwar (2010), Pfeffer (2010), Sackmann, Eggenhofer-Rehart/Friesl (2009), Worley/Feyerherm/Knudsen (2010).

29 An organization is defined here as a social system, which displays the characteristic of decision-making as self-referential communication. An organization exists when and as long as its autopoiesis continues, that is, decisions are reproduced from decisions. Through the occurrence of decision-making, organizations are reducers of complexity of social uncertainty.

30 See further Baecker (2007b), Beck (1986), Luhmann (2006), Spindler & Steger (2008)

31 Cf. Luhmann 2006, Spindler 2012 and following the idea that modern society has increased in complexity due to the loss of norms which were previously narrowly set by family and religion, states, etc. (Beck (1986).

32 Both are termed "environment" in system theory.

sonal responsibility, and approaches which are oriented to the world and designed to change society.

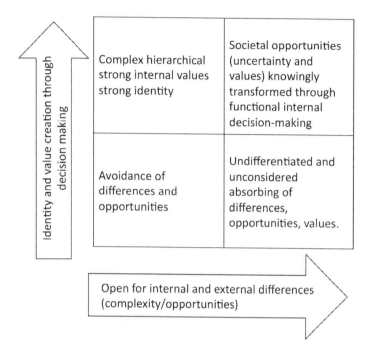

Figure 6: Organizations as transformers of uncertainty and values in society

The more dynamic and thus more complex the environment becomes (keyword: globalization and IT), the more important it becomes to have a conscious and functional development of the internal organization as an interweaving of decisions, which can counter this dynamic with a reflective flexibility. The decision for this development can only be made by the organization itself.

Making various communication patterns (structures, processes) useful for the desired purpose (the goals, the future, the identity and the values) is a central task for leadership. How an organization keeps itself alive depends on the abilities of its leadership system to be adequately and functionally aware of decision-making and its sense-making for the organization's identity by managing its borders to the environment. The "correct" multiple perspectives of perception and the process-structural arrangement of decisions (and thus also demarcation) are pivotal questions for sustainable leadership.

Principle 7: Leadership capacity as critically dealing with paradoxes and functionality

An organization's functional leadership system reflectively embraces all possible (hybrid) structures and leadership concepts and is able to put them in place as functionally needed. It uses structural concepts from hierarchy through network and hybrid leadership concepts[33]. The logic of homoeostasis is in the foreground. The intention is to keep the actions of others and their otherness in balance, assess them on the basis of superordinate common goals, and steer them by regulating conditions inter-independently, e.g. by (shared) decision-making and structuring, both limiting as well as enabling. Peripheral matters and risks (e.g. societal requirements) are taken into account reflectively, determining structure as a functional necessity.

When leadership systems are investigated, functional questions can be asked: Which structures, which kind of leadership and which cultures will help us to move as a whole toward our future? Situational, functional, and structural aspects influence each other in the realization of different structural forms[34]. More fragmented, hybrid and segmented organizations with greater diversity of structures and cultural and communication patterns require greater reflection, active design or creation, and integration of those multiple structures and communication patterns. A 'helicopter perspective' enables them to gain an overview and see the entire picture[35], including society.

Circular connections that reflect on themselves allow leadership to recognize the context and enable the actively formed development of an uncertain future in an uncertain context. Customized products can then be created with clients and simultaneously flow into the self-concept of the organization. This leads to increasingly fragmented organizational patterns. The organizational parts and individuals can no longer be explicitly classifiable; leadership responsibilities must constantly be newly and functionally created. A complex leadership system that keeps its sights fixed on conditions, possibilities and limits moves to the fore. Functional, customized,

---

33 See further leadership and intervention concepts such as linear – circular, trivial and non-trivial (Förster 1988), management and leadership (Kotter 2005), technical and adaptive leadership and organizations (Heifitz/Grashow/Linsky 2009), or in German: Führung und Steuerung, linear und systemisch (Malik 2002 and Spindler/Steger 2008).
34 See also Strikwerda/Stoelhorst (2009).
35 Spindler, M./Steger, M. (2008).

long-term, future-orientated, mutual formation with all its differences gains importance. Thus leadership becomes a feat to be accomplished by the managers working together.

In practice the first step is often the establishment of a leadership team and culture, which then develop a leadership concept, so that the unit and its identity can comprehend the differences, and the balance and transformation of those differences can be guaranteed. Developing towards a dynamic, uncertain future asks of and helps leadership on the one hand consciously to demarcate the organization (keywords: decision for strategic development and identity formation) and on the other to open it to general societal developments beyond a focus on current clients and markets, thus requiring a dynamic image of the complete organization and its paradoxes[36] for a customized and uncertain organizational future.

Conclusions: Collaborative leadership learning allows social sustainability for organizations for an uncertain future

If the attempt to build mutual capacity for abstraction is successful, situations can be investigated, observed, interpreted and changed. This means that observation and change can take place from different vantage points between various parts, thus taking complexity into consideration and making use of diversity. We are speaking here of:

- a collaborative leadership system which transforms contradictory truths and pours them into various communication patterns like structures in a dynamic image without dissolving the contradictions;
- a reflective image of organization and leadership from an observation perspective, in order to be able to recognize the diverse perspectives in their interconnections;
- a self-perception of leadership that refers to the increasing dynamic of the environment and the increased internal dynamic of the organization with which it is linked, and which uses the borders between organizational identity and inward-directed environmental activity as learning.

---

36 Cf. Oscillation of paradoxes in organizations by Littmann/Jansen (2000).

This communitized learning is necessary so that the leadership of an organization can grasp the dynamic environment and the future of that organization, even though the future is uncertain. This requires a reflective self-concept by leadership that equips them for an uncertain outcome of their own management actions in an uncertain environment and future. By critically questioning communitized leadership equipment, the transition from the 'modern' into the 'next society' in and through organizations can be consciously steered. Leadership as an entity can become a designer of the organization and of society.

Table of Figures

Figure 1: Action Circle – according to Lewin

Figure 2: Communitized abstraction

Figure 3: Taking functional self-responsibility

Figure 4: Vibrating of boundaries between system and environment

Figure 5: Functional abstraction

Figure 6: Organizations as transformers of uncertainty and values in society

Literature

Ashkenas, R./Ulrich, D., Jick, T./Kerr, S. (1992), The boundaryless organization: Breaking the chains of organizational structure. Jossey-Bass, San Francisco.
Baecker, D. (2005), Kommunikation. Reclam, Stuttgart.
Baecker, D. (2007a), Form und Formen der Kommunikation. Suhrkamp, Frankfurt/Main.
Baecker, D. (2007b), Studien zur nächsten Gesellschaft. Suhrkamp, Frankfurt/Main.
Baecker, D. (2009), Organisation als temporale Form: Ein Ausblick. In: Wimmer, R./Meissner, J. O./Wolf, P. (Eds.): Praktische Organisationswissenschaft. Carl-Auer, Heidelberg.
Bateson, G. (1979), Mind and Nature, A Necessary Unity, Bantam Books, Toronto, New York.
Beck, U. (1986), Risikogesellschaft. Auf dem Weg in eine andere Moderne. Suhrkamp, Frankfurt/Main.
Förster, H. von (1988), Abbau und Aufbau. In: Simon, F. (Ed.) (1997) Lebende Systeme. Wirklichkeitskonstruktionen in der systemischen Therapie. Suhrkamp, Frankfurt/Main.
Förster, Heinz von (1985), Sicht und Einsicht. Versuche zu einer operativen Erkenntnistheorie. Vieweg, Braunschweig,.
Haugh, H. M./Talwar, A., How do corporations embed sustainability across the organization? In: *Academy of Management Learning & Education*, 2010, 9 (3), 384–396.
Heifitz, R./Grashow, A./Linksky, M. (2009), The Practice of Adaptive Leadership. Harvard Business School Publishing.
Kotter, J. (2005), Cultures and Coalitions. In: Toffler, Alvi/Toffler, Heidi. Rethinking the Future. Nicholas Brealey Publishing, London, 164–178.
Littmann, P./Jansen, S. (2000), Oszillodox. Virtualisierung. Die permanente Neuerfindung der Organisation. Klett-Cotta, Stuttgart.
Luhmann, N. (1986), Soziale Systeme. Suhrkamp, Frankfurt/Main.

Luhmann, N. (2006), Organisation und Entscheidung (2nd edition). VS Verlag, Wiesbaden.
Malik, F. (2008), Strategie des Managements komplexer Systeme (10th edition) Haupt, Bern.
Marshall, S./Vaiman, V./Napier, N./Taylor, S./Häselberger, A./Andersen, T. (2010), The End of a 'Period': Sustainability and the Question Attidude. *Academy of Management Learning & Education*, 2010, 9 (3), 477–487.
McCarthy, D. J./Puffer, S. M. /Darda S. V. (2010), Convergence in Entrepreneurial Leadership Style: Evidence from Russia. *California Management Review*, 52 (4), 48–72.
Morgan, G. (2006), Images of Organization (Updated Edition of the International Bestseller) Sage Publications, Tousand Oaks, London, New Delhi.
Pfeffer, J. (2010), Building sustainable organizations: The human factor. In: *Academy of Management Perspectives*, Feb 2010, 24 (1), 34–45.
Puffer, S. M./McCarthy, D. J. (2011), Two Decades of Russian Business and Management Research. An Institutional Theory Perspective. Academy of Management Perspectives, Briarcliff Manor, NY.
Rerup, C./Feldman, M. S. (2011), Routines as a source of change in organizational schemata: The role or trial-and-error learning. In: *Academy of Management Journal*. June 2011. Vol. 54, No. 3, 577–610.
Sackmann, S. A./Eggenhofer-Rehart, P. M./Friesl, M. (2009), Sustainable change: Long-term efforts toward developing a learning organization. In: *Journal of Applied Behavioral Science*, 2009, 45 (4), 521–549.
Scharmer, Otto (2009), Theory U. Leading from the Future at It Emerges. Berret-Koehler, San Francisco.
Schein, E. (1997), Organisational Culture and Leadership (2nd edition). Jossey-Bass, San Francisco.
Schneider, S. C. (1987), Managing Boundaries in Organizations. In: *Political Psychology.* Vol. 8, No. 3, 1987.
Schwarz, G. (2007), Die „Heilige Ordnung" der Männer. Hierarchie, Gruppendynamik und die neue Rolle der Frauen. Verlag für Sozialwissenschaften, Wiesbaden.
Senge. P. (2006), The Fifth Discipline The art and practice of the learning organization. (revised edition). Doubleday, New York, NY.
Spindler, M. (2010), Projects as an Opportunity to Drive Lasting Organisational Learning. (Paper, 20 pages) *M/O/T – International Conference: "Management makes the world go round"*, December 1–4. 2010, online publication: http://www.iff.ac.at/oe/content.php?p=34&lang=mot&nr=
Spindler, M. (2012), How to awaken the potential of organizations to act as societal transformers. In: *Challenging Organisations and Society.* 2012, Vol. 1 (1).
Spindler, M./Steger, M. (2008), Metamangement in gebildeten Unternehmen. VDM, Saarbrücken.
Spindler, M./Steger, M. (2011), Management Consulting as Professional Helping. (Paper 20 Pages) In: *Academy of Management (AOM) Conference*, June 2011, Amsterdam.
Strikwerda, J./Stoelhorst, J. W. (2009), The Emergence and Evolution of the Multidimensional Organization. In: *California Management Review*, 51(4), 11–31.
Weik, K. E./Sutcliffe, K. E. (2001), Managing the Unexpected. Jossey-Bass, San Francisco.
Willke, H. (2007), Wissensgesellschaft. Kollektive Intelligenz und die Konturen eines kognitiven Kapitalismus. In: Pahl, H. & Meyer, L. (Eds.), Kognitiver Kapitalisums. Soziologische Beiträge zur Theorie der Wissensökonomie, p. 195–221. Metropolis-Verlag, Marburg.
Wimmer, R. (2009), Organisation als Differenz: Grundzüge eines systemtheoretischen Organisationsverständnisses. In: Wimmer, R./Meissner, J. O./Wolf, P. (Eds.), Praktische Organisationswissenschaft. Carl-Auer, Heidelberg.
Worley, C. G./Feyerherm, A. E./Knudsen, D. (2010), Building a collaboration capability for sustainability: How Gap Inc. is creating and leveraging a strategic asset. In: *Organizational Dynamics* (2010) 39, 325–334.

Maria Spindler

What leaders can learn through the case study process

As a Master's thesis advisor I often heard from students when they had finished their work: "I've learned so much about my corporation and about myself through this case study. It was really hard work, and it paid off for me." I like this feedback, as it shows that being pushed out of the comfort zone and well-known habits can enable learning. And yes, through research case process studies leaders can learn to observe more complex and to question dysfunctional standards. They are invited to see their organisation and themselves from an observer's position. The learning process provides an overview that supports understanding of organisational patterns, the sedimentation of structures and processes over time, and thus the history of an organisation as a "solution-finding machine" for past problems. The history of decision-making and past consequences can be explored, and influences for the future can be interpreted. Observation as the first step of the action cycle is essential for leadership action: because what leaders cannot see, they also cannot interpret, plan or change.[1]

1 Observation and questioning as learning provocations for complex systems

The student as practitioner is interwoven with a complex self-steering system and thus obtains insight into its logic and his or her own point of view. The ability to reflect and the learning that occurs become the starting point for his or her own learning and changes of the whole system. Therefore it is essential for the practitioner to be clear about his or her own different functions, for example line management, internal consultant, project manager or researcher for the practitioner's own case study, and their interplay: From which perspective do I observe and interpret my actions at this moment? What is my goal from each of my perspectives? From which perspectives do I want to observe? In which context am I interwoven in which function?

---

[1] See the action cycle in Spindler (2013) in this book.

One of the reasons the concept of case studies is powerful is that practitioners have to question their own daily business and see the mutual interplay within complex living systems[2]. They learn to observe and question patterns like leadership and corporate culture, structures and strategy, within their area of accountability and beyond. In other words, they are expected to deal with functionality, to have an idea where to use which structure, which style of leadership communication and which culture in order to support innovation and transformation in organisations[3]. They have the opportunity to become aware of different action-logics and connect them to the adequate contexts.

As self-steering and self-observing systems, organisations develop ways that influence their future through their own process of self-observation as they are learning systems. How complexly they are able to perceive themselves has a great impact on their actions and development. This also depends on how people, departments, leaders, and employees observe them. The various self-observations within a social system and the differences in individual impressions are important elements for creating social realities[4].

Case studies[5] can enable leaders simultaneously to become critical observers and learners about their own observation patterns on their complex organised situations: communication patterns like organisational, cultural and leadership mindsets and actions. Organisations are self-observing systems, learning systems that develop ways to influence their future through the process of self-observation. How they (their leaders) perceive themselves has a great impact on their actions and the development of their organisations. The complex requirements for interventions by leadership depend on the leaders' ability to focus on the complexity of the organisation as a living system[6].

In this research case study approach the special learning focus is the discovery and understanding of the company's organisations and leadership potential from the company's previously developed learning capabilities. This is a way of enabling practitioners to gain new action-logics for themselves. This way of learning is designed for professionals who are reflective and down-to-earth in their adult leadership life. This program emphasises

---

2 Cf. Spindler (2013), Spindler/Steger (2008, p. 512 ff.) and Malik (2003).
3 Cf. further Spindler (2013).
4 Cf. Grossmann/Scala (2012).
5 I had the pleasure of developing these over years together with the "Center for Journalism and Communication Management".
6 Cf. Grossmann/Scala (2012).

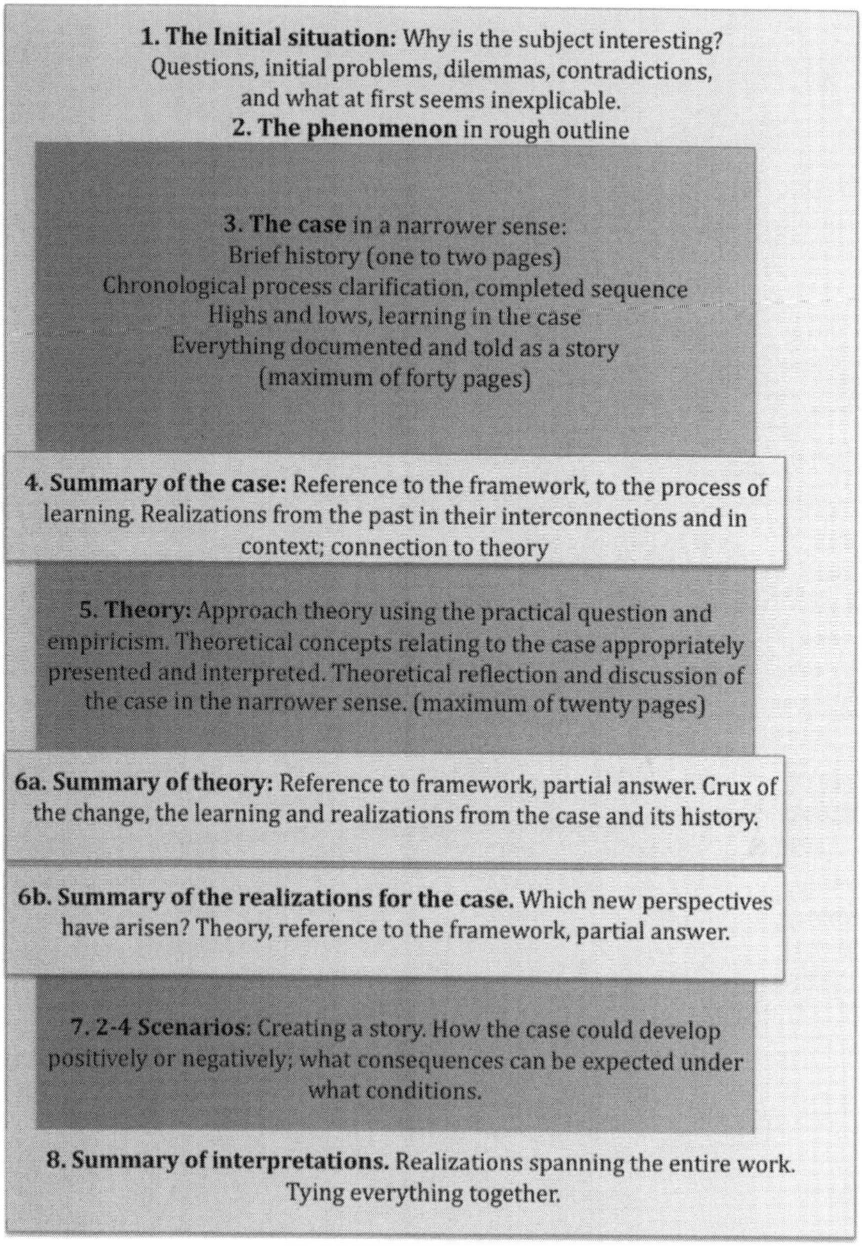

1. The Initial situation: Why is the subject interesting? Questions, initial problems, dilemmas, contradictions, and what at first seems inexplicable.
2. The phenomenon in rough outline

3. The case in a narrower sense:
Brief history (one to two pages)
Chronological process clarification, completed sequence
Highs and lows, learning in the case
Everything documented and told as a story
(maximum of forty pages)

4. Summary of the case: Reference to the framework, to the process of learning. Realizations from the past in their interconnections and in context; connection to theory

5. Theory: Approach theory using the practical question and empiricism. Theoretical concepts relating to the case appropriately presented and interpreted. Theoretical reflection and discussion of the case in the narrower sense. (maximum of twenty pages)

6a. Summary of theory: Reference to framework, partial answer. Crux of the change, the learning and realizations from the case and its history.

6b. Summary of the realizations for the case. Which new perspectives have arisen? Theory, reference to the framework, partial answer.

7. 2-4 Scenarios: Creating a story. How the case could develop positively or negatively; what consequences can be expected under what conditions.

8. Summary of interpretations. Realizations spanning the entire work. Tying everything together.

Diagram 1: Overview of the sections of a Master's thesis[7]

---

[7] Spindler (2010).

the learning opportunities between leadership practice and theory. The developed case study concept emphasises the learning with/from one's own experience. By the end of the fourth program[8] we had developed a vast array of material designed to support and guide the practitioners in writing their cases, to help them open themselves by widening their perspectives for the past and the future of their own situations and opportunities for their company. The following structure supports the practitioners as a guideline through their work for their own situations.

The initial situation (see steps 1 and 2 above) is crucial, creating a case study as such and positioning oneself as an author within the case. The students explore and define their main interests and the phenomena connected to the case system and its borders. The instructors pay special attention to emotional involvement and hidden agendas. It is the definition phase of the heart of the story, the phenomena, their interconnections and their limits, an essential step for the practitioners in order to own their own stories and be motivated throughout the entire case study process: one's own research case study as one's own questions asked, the story told (see storytelling) within a timeframe, preferably using a graphic showing the 'inciting incident' that throws the life of the system (and one's own life) out of balance. Where does the story start? What are my assumptions, motivations and involvements as a leader, which seem to be the driving forces for taking a closer look at this story? Definition of the research question and/or assumption: In this step the researchers decide what should be investigated in detail and why.

The case (see Step 3): includes a) the history of the story, e.g. foundations, mergers, the story of failure and learning, etc., b) the present context of the core case, for instance leadership culture, structural mindsets, values, strategic perspectives, technical requirements, competitors, changes in the law, etc. c) The core story is classified by topic and made comprehensible for the reader (see further below the elaborations of "storytelling" and "research for oneself and others"). The practitioners are challenged to think in different action-logics, multiple systems and frameworks, which are supposed to be in accordance with the requirements of the leadership situation.

For the *theoretical part* (see Step 5) the practitioners are advised to use theory as a reflecting tool for their cases. Theory helps them to step further back from their own involvement and to observe and interpret more complexly and deeply than before. The development of *two to four scenarios* (see Step 7) makes this organisational learning the focus once more, because the

---

8   In 2011, see also Ettl-Huber/Bauer (2013) in this book.

organisational context for the learning phenomenon is de-familiarised. Thus the practitioner is forced to define the core of what is learned and to verify it for the changed context: to what extent can organisational learning stand up to changed contexts? The leader's capability of abstraction in relation to organisational learning is honed further. The *summary and interpretations* (see Step 8) embrace the entire case study and sum up the challenges and changes of this qualitative empirical scientific work.

Examples of Master's thesis case study topics are:
- Merger as the motivation for the move from extended workbench to independent company.
- How the concept of the learning organisation can be put into practice in the X department of the Y bank.
- The consolidation of seven professional associations into one umbrella organisation.

2 Case studies as opportunities for further adult learning for practitioners

Supporting practitioners through this process of writing case studies is a certain form of providing an environment for the opportunity to develop leadership capacity further. Conventional MBA programs are almost exclusively designed for young people with little, if any, leadership experience. The programs overemphasize science in the form of analysis and technique and downplay experience and insight. As a result, graduates leave with a distorted impression that leadership consists entirely of applying formulas in order to solve complex situations[9]. Case studies can serve as one key element to interlink leadership practice and adult learning. The following approaches are helpful:

2.1 Telling one's own story to challenge oneself

In my experience as a thesis advisor, using the concept of storytelling provides access to the story behind the practitioner's story and encourages in-

---

9 Mintzberg (2004) argues that this way of teaching MBA-students has had a corrupting and dehumanising effect not just on the practice of management, but also on our business world, the non-profit sector and community organisations, and even our social and cultural institutions.

vestigation of learning within the case and for the case writer him or herself. They are advised to tell the story in a way that moves the storyteller and potential readers. Focusing on an 'inciting incident' and 'lessons learned' according to the concept of Robert McKee[10] is very helpful. So the story begins with a situation in which the organisational life is in balance and is then thrown out of balance by an 'inciting incident'. Practitioners are advised to tell their story within a certain timeframe in which a dramatic change forced the organisations and their leaders to act. Providing a timeline as a graphic illustrating the main impacts and main changes clarifies the students' thinking and helps them to stay in line and keep focused. With a focus on storytelling as narrative and an inductive approach, the students are advised to jump into the field, start collecting data and writing their story[11]. The practitioner uses interviews to obtain multiple perspectives on critical points. He/she perceives and comprehends different interests and contexts, achieving a necessary distance from existing personal patterns of observation and interpretation. The respective phenomena in leadership and organisation are explored and translated into a language comprehensible to all involved stakeholders and other interested parties. In so doing the researcher contributes to the wellbeing of different stakeholders in relation to their organisation.

2.2 Systemised learning from the past for the future

While looking into the past and telling the story about the problem-solving process as the core of the case study, a variation of Kurt Lewin's circle serves as one of the main sources for the action research approach: Observation-Interpretation-Planning-Implementing. The assumption is that research results will be more valuable if they have already been tested as implemented solutions for the ‚inciting incident'. The knowledge is already tested; it is not just a plan or criticism of a current situation, as the resulting learning is derived from solutions already implemented. Thus the writer and reader can be certain that the plan did (not) work in that specific case and can be useful (or not) for other cases in similar contexts.[12]

Through the systemised story with observation, interpretation, planning and implementation, the feedback from colleagues and instructors, and the

---

10 McKee (2003).
11 See further Czarniawska's concept of storytelling (2006).
12 See further the topic of generalisation in case studies at Spindler/Steger (2013).

reflection on theory, the past can be seen anew. Present and future perspectives can change and lead to different interpretations, planning and implementing for the next incident.

2.3 The laboratory situation enables transformation

One can say that the MBA Program provides a learning laboratory[13]. The student is forced to look into his or her own situation at greater depth and focus. This leaves room in his or her mind for other approaches, logics, interests and experiences.[14]

Giving and receiving feedback supports this development.[15] On the one hand the action focus is laid on the practitioner's own motives, explanations and incentives; on the other hand a link is created between the organised system[16] and the various interests. The laboratory situation enables detours, trial and error, both emotional and cognitive, which can lead to irritation and room for other cognitive and emotional perception and maneuver.

Therewith practitioners move into an in-depth, holistic understanding of themselves in connection with their own business environment. In terms of Rooke and Torbert, this process provides the context and opportunity for transformation[17] from the action- logic of the 'conventional achiever' to the 'post-conventional individualist' who is able to interweave competing personal and company action-logics.[18]

It is crucial that the practitioners are ready to take the risk of failure and learning, as this laboratory situation is fraught with risk and difficulty for the individual. At the same time they reach beyond themselves, dedicated to questioning their own assumptions by widening their awareness. The person seeking to exercise transforming power must seek challenges to his/her ap-

---

13　Cf. Ettl-Huber/Bauer (2013).
14　Cf. Bauer (2013), From individual learning to organisational learning – findings of interviews.
15　Cf. Bauer/Ettl-Huber (2013).
16　The system can exhibit various borders: the team, the specialist field, the department, the whole organisation, etc., in their respective environments and contexts.
17　Transformation refers not to horizontal learning but to vertical development, which usually brings with it a crisis situation which questions patterns that have been practiced for years. They describe the various action-logics as Opportunist, Diplomat, Expert, Achiever, Individualist, Strategist, and Alchemist (Rooke/Torbert, 2005, p. 69).
18　Cf. Torbert (2010), Rooke/Torbert (2005) and Fischer, Rooke & Torbert (2003).

proach in every way possible – by taking on dilemmas within the awareness of increasing complexity, dilemmas that go more deeply to the heart of the culture as a whole, or by discovering new ways of changing perspectives that show the consequences of his or her former or current perspective and action.

It provides the context for a transformation, a leap into the 'post-conventional' action- logic where leaders gain the opportunity to question given values, structures, processes and patterns. This is a first step into creating unique structures to resolve gaps between strategy and performance. Different truths, dilemmas, contradictions and possible conflicts between perspectives are part of the awareness[19].

3 Research for one's own practice, science and others

Advisor experience on Master's theses has shown that a case study can become a comprehensive approach that makes the unexamined visible when:

- The practitioner who is emotionally entangled receives support from a group of researchers and instructors. This assistance helps the researcher to detach and step back in order to gain the necessary distance for his or her own perception and action.
- A research diary is used to absorb emotional pressure so that it can be processed or worked through.
- Practitioners experience theory as a useful exploratory and descriptive tool. In this way a case study can be seen as an emancipating approach which generates knowledge and opportunities for development:
  – For researchers and their own practice as managers
  – For companies and their staff
  – For other organisations and for academic research.

A case study process makes the practitioner a living instrument. It both enables and requires using his/her interest and opens the door to his/her learning. Thus the practitioners can be seen as living resources who provide access to leadership and organisational phenomena and their connections.

---

19 What this means for leadership requirements and capacity you can read in detail in Spindler (2013) in this book: Spindler, M. (2013), Organizations and their Interplay with Leadership for an Uncertain Future.

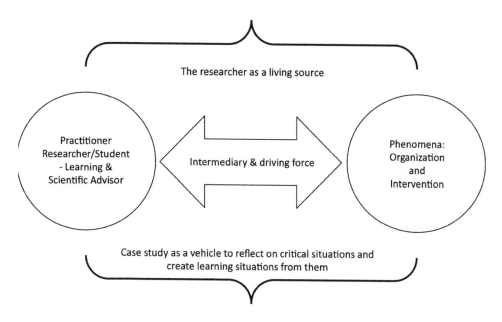

Diagram 2: The researcher as a living source[20]

This accessibility exists both inside and outside the organisation, for science as well as for other leaders. Through this reflected interest, hidden phenomena and critical points of interventions into organisations become delimited and accessible for research.

Practice has shown that a case study where emotional aspects are included and consciously used becomes a rich and highly reflective technique and product. In such a case, organisations as well as the people living and working in them gain new access to the phenomena of organisations and management. Against the background of the interplay of different interpretations and interests, the culture of learning receives the central focus it deserves.

4 Conclusions: Expand the capacity for learning

Learning and capacity building are no coincidences. The learning potential of case studies can be planned and supported in various ways and requires a

---

20 Based on the developments of Spindler/Schmerold (2010, p. 2).

conscious decision on the concept of learning. The central point of the approach presented here is to expand leadership capacity for organisational learning from the past in order to use it for oneself and the organisation as a new set of actions for future learning challenges. The company's leadership and organisational action from the past becomes systematised in the form of observations, interpretations, planning and implementations and is seen from a stricter learning orientation. As an approach for creating a distance and new perspectives into the past the case study results in new opportunities for actions in the future.

In a research case study the focus changes from an emotionally involved leadership position to a researcher's perspective; this role change is based on the practitioner's obligation to find and use sources through which emotions and actions are scientifically justified. The shift of the focus is:

- From daily business and emotional patterns to well-grounded, reasonable interpretations;
- From self-centralised observation to observing from a 'third perspective' which includes and improves the system perspective;
- From a hands-on to a hands-off attitude towards analysing leadership within the organisational development and context.

It provides a critically observed leadership situation seen through different perspectives, questioning organisational learning from the past in order to use it for oneself and the organisation as a new set of action-logics for future learning challenges.

The focus changes from a personal, emotionally involved position to a holistic qualitative research perspective; this role change is based on leadership's obligation to find and use sources through which emotions and actions are scientifically justified and told as a scientific story for others: a complex, scientific story of different truths, dilemmas, contradictions and possible conflicts between different perspectives, a process and result of learning and change. Hence a case study is a living contribution enabling leaders to move more effectively within a constantly changing environment and that can be added to their repertoire of observations as a basis for more opportunities to act within complex living systems and thereby create a future for all of us.

Literature

Bauer, E. M. (2013), Case studies: definition, application, strengths. What is a case study? In: Spindler, M./ Bauer, E. M. (Eds.), Research Case Studies as Learning Challenges for Leaders and Organisations. Verlagshaus Hernals, Vienna.

Bauer, E. M. (2013), From individual learning to organisational learning – findings of interviews, In: Spindler, M./Bauer, E. M. (Eds.), Research Case Studies as Learning Challenges for Leaders and Organisations. Verlagshaus Hernals, Vienna.

Czarniawska, B. (2006), Narratives in Social Research. Sage Publications, London.

Ettl-Huber, S./Bauer, E. M. (2013), Supervision of Students in the Case Study Process – an elaborated support process for mastering case studies. In: Spindler, M./ Bauer, E. M. (Eds.), Research Case Studies as Learning Challenges for Leaders and Organisations. Verlagshaus Hernals, Vienna.

Fischer, D./Rooke, D./Torbert, B. (2003), Personal and Organisational Transformations Through Action Inquiry (Revised 4th edition). Edge/Work Press, Boston.

Grossmann, R./Scala, K. (2012), Organisational Consulting and Development In: Facilitating Collaboration in Public Management.

Malik, F. (2008), Strategie des Managements komplexer Systeme (10th. edition), Haupt, Bern.

McKee, R. (2003), Storytelling - That Moves People In: Harvard Business Review, June 2003, R0306D.

Mintzberg, H. (2004), Managers not MBAs. A hard look at the soft practise of managing and the development of managers. Berret-Koehler, San Francisco.

Rooke, D./Torbert, B. (2005), Seven Transformations of Leadership. *Harvard Business Review* 4, 2005.

Spindler, M. (2010), Einführung in Case Study. (Teaching Material, Introduction to Case Study), Vienna.

Spindler, M. (2013), Organisations and its Interplay with Leadership for an Uncertain Future. Seven Principles. In Spindler, M./Bauer, E.M. (Eds.), Research Case Studies as Learning Challenges for Leaders and Organisations. Verlagshaus Hernals, Vienna.

Spindler, M./Schmerold, K. (2010), Proposal for the paper for the MOT Conference. Vienna.

Spindler, M./Steger, M. (2013), The scientific methodology of research case studies. In Spindler, M./Bauer, E. M. (Eds.), Research Case Studies as Learning Challenges for Leaders and Organisations. Verlagshaus Hernals, Vienna.

Torbert, B. (2010), Toward Development of Politics and the Political. *Integral Review*, March 2010, Vol. 6, No. 1.

Silvia Ettl-Huber . Eva Maria Bauer

Supervision of students in the case study process – An elaborated support process for mastering case studies

In recent years the supervision of students preparing their Master's theses has become a core task for those responsible at the Center for Journalism and Communication Management. In addition to continual efforts at improvement, two external developments increase in its importance: on the one hand the public discussion of plagiarism and the overall quality of academic papers, and on the other hand the simple transparency of such papers, the full texts of which can now be accessed through the library. The era in which inferior papers could be hidden in the lower shelves of the library has ended.

The situation at the Danube University Krems with its orientation to part-time students who are simultaneously professionally active is specific. On the one hand, through their professional activities the students have excellent access to information from practical experience; on the other hand, the time they have available to write their Master's theses is extremely limited. In addition, the students' previous academic training varies widely. Some have already written one or more theses while others have achieved an equivalent qualification entitling them to enter university study and are completely new to the challenge of writing scientific papers.

The academically experienced students, however, also display great differences in the quality of their previous training. In addition, when writing their Master's theses they often come upon completely different sources – for example from the natural sciences – and must first learn to deal with the requirements of a Master's thesis in the social sciences or economics. It was therefore necessary to design a style of supervision for widely different starting points, which still allowed a high degree of standardization. This standardization is of special importance because students at the Center for Journalism and Communication Management enter a program, which is designed for groups of up to twenty students who will all complete their theses at the same time.

In the specific case of supervision of the students of the MBA programme Communication and Leadership, it was assumed during the first presentation of the course of study that the students were able to work relatively independently but should be tied to a fixed framework. With support from course documents the students were introduced to the material of the case study. For further support, guidelines were developed to direct students through the case study process. A timeline[1] was distributed to the students and discussed with them, serving as an orientation to the milestones and the points in time at which they had to be completed. Another part of this first conversation was a briefing on academic papers by the seminar and course leader. There were a total of two informal meetings between the course leader, Master's thesis supervisor and students; the goal of these meetings was also to build peer groups to motivate the students: they were asked to form groups with others working on similar themes so that they could support each other, regularly exchange ideas and learn from each other.

The results from the first year's group of students, who received this type of support, were presentable but showed room for improvement. Dealing with documents and the back-to-front process of academic writing, in which questions were first developed before links in the literature were sought, caused difficulties for the students. Especially those students who had already written a Master's thesis in the usual style for an academic thesis had to free themselves from the old pattern; not all of them succeeded in this, which resulted in mixed forms of case study and traditional Master's thesis.

In later courses the supervision process was continuously improved and intensified. The essential principles were:

- Continuous exchange between supervisor and student
- Exchange of ideas among the students led by the course directors (directed peer group learning)
- Milestone principle through clearly specified timelines
- Despite intensive supervision, full responsibility for text, documents and procedure rests with the student

Experience showed that self-organised learning did not take place in combination with professional stress and the requirements of the course of study. The idea of peer group learning had to be declared a failure. Because the principle of evaluating and learning from the work of others was still considered to be indispensable, it was actively integrated into the seminars, which were then introduced.

---

1 Bauer (2006) Timeline Professional MBA Communication and Leadership.

Responsibility for supervision of the case studies was mostly shared between two people: the seminar facilitator, who held an appropriate academic qualification (at least a doctorate) and the director of the course of study. The director also serves as the first advisor for the completed Master's thesis and signs for the successful completion of the Master's thesis process. The seminar facilitator serves as the second thesis advisor and supports the director. Together they are responsible for the success of the complete course of study.

Today the supervision process of the case study Master's thesis consists of the following points:

1 The process of finding a subject

The process of finding a subject usually begins before the course of study. Course applicants must complete a questionnaire in order to come up with a representative case. During the admission interview the applicant is asked to discuss two subjects: first, his or her motivation for taking part in the course and second, the proposed case. In a one-on-one interview applicant and director discuss the following points:

- The suitability of the proposed case
- The questionnaire
- The planned time period of the case investigation
- Quality and quantity of the available empirical material

2 Three seminars on case studies[2]

- First academic seminar:

The seminar is designed to be interactive. It consists of an introduction to the case study process by the seminar facilitator and a first presentation of the planned case studies by the students as well as feedback from both the other students and the seminar facilitator and the course director. The facilitator especially emphasizes that the students should also deal with the other cases; therefore each student is assigned an alter ego who, according

---

2 Bauer (2012) Timeline Case Study.

to guidelines,[3] gives feedback on the concept of the case. The rest consists of free feedback from the group.

- Second academic seminar:

In the second seminar the students present the first twenty pages of the case study description. The feedback loops in this seminar are also designed so that the first feedback comes from another student designated by the seminar facilitator; then the facilitator, director and other students make their observations. The feedback is based on criteria in the evaluation system for the academic seminar. The suggestions are worked into the composition and submitted for evaluation.

- Third academic seminar:

The researchers present the status quo or the progress of the case. They should now have written at least the maximum forty pages of the case as well as the first theoretical input, a maximum of 20 pages. This material is again presented in front of an audience (the other student researchers and their instructors). The presentation and critical feedback by the seminar facilitator and director as well as that of the study colleagues again forces the researchers to explain as precisely as possible. These suggestions are again worked into the composition and submitted for evaluation.

It became clear that many questions could be answered during the seminar, from simple tips on citations to new formulation of questions. The advantage for the supervisor is in the expenditure of time, which is significantly less than that required for individual consultations. In addition, an improvement in the quality of the teaching content was observed, because within the full group far more sweeping questions were asked than in individual consultations.

Despite the advantages of group learning in the seminar, there are also limitations related to the size of the group. It has become clear that in groups of seven or more the potential learning effects can be exhausted because the problems and questions tend to become repetitive. Every member of the group has the chance for feedback on his or her specific topic and the right to receive attention; a maximum manageable size of ten participants was set in order to guarantee the attention of the group. This means that in practice any group of course participants of eleven or more is divided into two.

---

3   Bauer/Ettl-Huber/Spindler (2012) Evaluation System Case Study.

3 Feedback loops for the Master's thesis

During the academic seminars the students are supervised through the completion of the empirical part of the case study. In each seminar the progress on the paper and the basic considerations are discussed. In preparation for the individual seminars, shorter compositions are submitted. Nevertheless, by the end of the seminar the supervisors have seen only excerpts of the Master's thesis. Before the thesis is submitted in its final form, the student is obligated to submit an unbound version.

This submission usually occurs one month before the final submission date so that the student still has the opportunity to work on the suggestions given. This feedback comes from the seminar facilitator and director in the form of written comments, which follow a fixed feedback[4] scheme and are based on the final evaluation criteria.

These criteria are:
1. The empirical case description: choice and limitation of subject, clarity of the problem posed and framework of the case, presentation of various perspectives including documentation (protocols, e-mails, etc.) and other sources (interviews with involved parties, etc.), insights gained, knowledge acquired from the previous solutions to the case.
2. Methodological procedure: structuring and differentiation of the contents relevant to the subject and the problem, treatment of relevant aspects of the subject in appropriate depth as well as the connections made and with respect to the background, the author's own positioning, argumentative interpretation and scientific-critical attitude on the basis of relevant sources, clear lines of argumentation, central theme, object, clear and comprehensible writing style, citations, bibliography, documentation, appendix.
3. External appearance: guidance for the reader, orthography, and layout.

If there are problems with the case study process, which are beyond the scope of the seminars, the students have the opportunity to schedule individual consultations with the supervisors.

The case study process ends with the approval certificates of both the seminar facilitator and director and the defence of the case study before an

---
4   Bauer/Ettl-Huber (2012) Sheet Feedback Case Study.

examination board. From the two approval certificates a maximum of seventy out of one- hundred possible points can be awarded. The examination board for the oral defence gives the remaining maximum of thirty points.

The case study process reaches from the preliminary formulation of the idea during the admission interview (usually one to three months before the course begins) through the entire course of study to the defence of the case study, lasting a total of thirteen to fifteen months. When one considers that during this time the students are full-time working professionals, complete modules at home and abroad and have examinations to sit, the preparation of a case study sounds almost utopic. Experience from courses conducted so far shows, however, that this effort is possible. The components that we have identified for its success are a fixed timeline, continuous seminars, group learning, feedback loops and individual mentoring.

References

Bauer, E. M. (2006), Timeline Professional MBA Communication and Leadership. Material is owned by Danube University Krems and not open to public access.
Bauer, E. M./Ettl-Huber, S./Spindler, M. (2012), Evaluation System Case Study. Material is owned by Danube University Krems and not open to public access.
Bauer, E. M./Ettl-Huber, S. (2012), Sheet Feedback Case Study. Material is owned by Danube University Krems and not open to public access.

Astrid Valek

How the concept of the learning organization can be put into practice

Taking as an example a department of the Raiffeisenbank Region Schwechat.

1 Introduction and overview

The following case uses the example of a department of the Raiffeisenbank to present the development of the process of organizational learning and the resulting concrete implementations. The Marketing Director's vision was the impulse and starting point for the development of a new culture in her department. She amalgamated her previous knowledge and ideal conceptions of a learning organization[1] with the requirement to put organizational learning into practice. The measures taken in the process and their consequences, especially their effects and interactions, are described below. Her central role as manager, designer, advisor and companion are illustrated. The change process which the Marketing Director herself passed through is also made clear.

The concept of the learning organization conformed to the intention of the Marketing Director and, upon closer observation, also to the ideas of her employees, who during the change worked with all their strength toward their common goal. She involved her employees from the start. Discussions were used for reflection; she dealt with resistance from outside; processes and structures were adapted and changed as needed.

The Marketing Director's vision[2] and the will for change associated with it enabled individual learning, team learning and organizational learning, and thus a continual advancement in the development of the target group "youth".

---

1 The current primary representative of the *learning organization* approach is Peter Senge, whose book *The Fifth Discipline – The Art and Practice of the Learning Organization* first appeared in 1990 and became a definitive work.
2 Cf. Marketing Director's journal entry of 28 October 2008, p. 1.

The chronology of the case can be represented as follows:

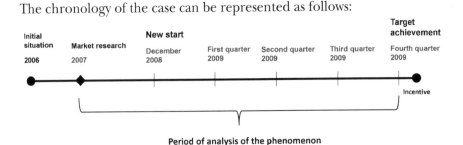

Figure 1: Time bar 2006–2009

The case comprises the time period from the middle of 2006 to the end of 2009 and describes how the concept of the learning organization was implemented. The effects of decisions and the consequences of actions are illustrated. Furthermore, the ways in which the team dealt with success and failure and their effects and consequences are presented.

2 Initial situation

2.1 The concept of the learning organization as a vision for the Marketing Director's own leadership

The *learning organization* is an organization which enables the learning of all members of the organization and which continually transforms itself.[3] P. Senge requires the renunciation of isolated thinking and behavior patterns in order to create a competitive advantage for the organization and its employees. It is not sufficient simply for individuals to learn in place of the organization. The organization of the future, the learning organization, is characterized by the fact that knowledge and learning potential are developed at all levels of the organization. According to Senge, organizations achieve this goal when they concentrate on five constitutive disciplines:

Personal Mastery: *the discipline of self-direction and personal development. People with a high degree of personal mastery continually expand their ability to achieve the results to which they truly aspire.*

Mental Models: *These are deeply rooted inner assumptions, generalizations or complex theories which steer our actions. Mental models very often hinder learning. In order to be overcome, they must be brought to the surface.*

---

3 Cf. Sattelberger 1995, p. 60. and Senge 2008, p. 14 ff.

Shared Vision: *When people share a vision they feel bonded, united by a common goal. A collective vision draws its strength from a deep common interest and provides energy for the learning organization.*

Team Learning: *Team Learning is a process through which a team continuously aligns and broadens its ability to achieve its desired goals. The discipline of team learning involves the mastery of the techniques of dialogue and discussion by those involved.*

Systems Thinking: *An absolute requirement for success is the interaction of the constituent disciplines, because success is only guaranteed by their interconnectedness. For this reason Senge calls systems thinking the decisive fifth discipline. It is the integrative discipline, which connects them all and knits them together into a holistic theory.*

The learning organization approach is characterized by three points: it emphasizes the holistic aspect of the company; it avows content-related problem solving on the basis of a continual learning process within the organization which involves all employees; and it allocates to managers the role of advisor and designer rather than authoritarian commander.

In 2006, based on her own experience, the Marketing Director was convinced that traditional leadership with clear hierarchies and direction was counterproductive to a learning organization. Managers in this approach are designers and advisors (Senge calls them "stewards")[4] responsible for development and collective learning, and as such they take on a role foreign to the organization's culture.

2.2 Initial situation of the bank in 2006

The Raiffeisenbank Region Schwechat is an independent, profitable regional bank with a closely-knit network of branches. On 31 December 2006 the Raiffeisenbank Region Schwechat reported a balance of € 399.4 million.[5] 21,538 customers were served by a staff of 126 and 1,649 of these customers were between 10 and 19 years of age.[6] The main branch is located in Schwechat; there are eleven further branches in the following locations: Enzersdorf, Fischamend, Flughafen Wien, Schwechat, Götzendorf, Himberg, Gramatneusiedl, Maria Lanzendorf, Mitterndorf, Reisenberg and Schwadorf.[7]

---

4 Cf. Senge: 2008, p. 410 ff.
5 Cf. Annual Statement of Accounts of the RB Schwechat of 31.12.2006, p. 1 ff.
6 Cf. Analysis Controlling: Development of the Number of Customers by Age Group, 2009.
7 Cf. Website of the RB Schwechat, www.rbschwechat.at.

Then as now the bank is divided into three strategic business areas, each of which is under the responsibility of a Managing Director:[8]

- Private customers
- Business customers
- Private banking for high net worth individuals (HNI)

Private customers represent the great majority (95%) of the total number of the bank's customers.[9] The "youth market"[10] is also assigned to the private customer business area. It is handled by thirteen youth advisors[11] in the bank and plays an important role in further development.

2.3 Interpreting urgency and recognizing it as potential for change

In 2006 the Raiffeisenbank Region Schwechat was facing stagnating growth in customer numbers[12], although the bank was located in a region into which more and more families were moving and whose population was growing between 10% and 15% annually[13]. The management recognized this danger. To analyze the cause(s), market research was commissioned by the Raiffeisenlandesbank NÖ-Wien in March 2007.

The result of the market research made clear that the Raiffeisenbank Region Schwechat's customer base showed a tendency toward aging. Due to demographic changes, both mortality rates and birth rates had sunk in recent years. For the Raiffeisenbank Region Schwechat this meant that their customers were becoming older and older, while too few new young custom-

---

8 Cf. Organizational Structure – Structural Organization of the RB Schwechat as of 30.11.2007.
9 Cf. Analysis Controlling: Development of the Number of Customers, Private Customers, Business Customers and Private Banking, 2009.
10 Target Group Segment children, pupils and students between the ages of 10 and 20 and students through the age of 25.
11 Each youth advisor works in one of the RB Schwechat's eleven branches, mostly in the service area, and is responsible for handling the youth market. In large branches there are two youth advisors. The focus of their activities is on gaining and supporting young bank customers – the acquisition of pocket money, youth and student accounts.
12 Cf. Analysis Controlling: Development of the Number of Active Customers, 2006.
13 Cf. Raiffeisenlandesbank NÖ-Wien: Market research. Population development 2001–2006, 2007.

ers were being added. This represented a risk for the bank which, while not immediate, would soon become grave.

Figure 2 illustrates the development most strikingly. It shows that in January 2003 (grey area) more new young customers had been obtained than in January 2007 (grey line).

The strong downward movement in the ages between 18 and 21 illustrates the loss of young customers: many new young customers were lost again when they turned twenty and their free youth account changed to a cost-incurring private account.

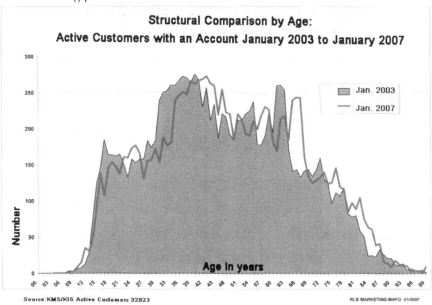

Figure 2: Structural comparison by age: Active customers with an account 2003–2007
Source: Raiffeisenlandesbank NÖ-Wien, Market research, 2007.

The management responded to the results of the market research as follows, proving the future orientation of their thinking and actions:

"The analysis of our customer structure clearly showed where the causes for the stagnation in our customer numbers lay and how important the development of the youth market was to a successful future for the Raiffeisenbank Region Schwechat."[14]

The results of the market analysis led the management to rethink. Their recognition that today's youth are the customers of tomorrow and as such are of essential importance for the bank began to gain importance in the

---

14 Interview 1, p. 1.

management's thinking. The youth market segment was recognized as strategically important. The following statement underlines this point:

"*This department is extremely important for the bank. New youth accounts and the resulting future transfer to adequate salary accounts ensure that the bank has a healthy basis for long-term growth*,"[15] was the management's conclusion.

Up to this point the youth market with the target customer group of children and youth had been neglected by the bank, even smiled at by some employees, since the bank only makes profit on young customers as soon as they turn twenty. Then they have to pay for their accounts.

3 Structural and personnel changes

As a first consequence of the market research results, the management changed the organizational assignment of the youth market: previously assigned to Sales, from November 2008 the assignment and responsibility for results were transferred to Marketing. A new manager, mentioned above, took over the strategic and organizational leadership of this area. The direct contact person for the thirteen colleagues (youth advisors) continued to be the Team Leader from Sales.

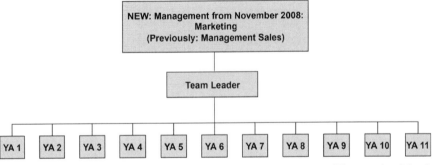

Figure 3: New structure in the youth market area   (YA = youth advisor)

The Marketing Director defined the assignments of the team as well as her own: the strategic, value-oriented, organizational steering and the responsibility for results lay with the Marketing Director; the operative implementation of the activities was assigned to the Team Leader, together with the employees and customers.[16] The close cooperation between the two

---

15   Interview 1, p. 2.
16   Cf. Duties and Responsibilities of the Market Director and Team Leader.

managers having been agreed upon, the style of communication in this management situation represented above all the key factor for success.

4 The Marketing Director's strategic realignment of the area

In the following months the Marketing Director changed the general framework and increased the significance of the area responsible for the acquisition and service of young customers by changing communication policies. Starting in January 2009 the Marketing Director reported weekly to various executive committees on the area's activities and results in order to sensitize the other managers. There was also an external realignment. The website was expanded to include a separate section for the youth market with photos of the employees and information on products. In this way the employees and their marketing activities received much more attention from all managers of the complete organization. The Marketing Director acted on the assumption that the youth advisors should be granted a decisive role in the handling of the market.[17]

In the 2006 marketing research the analysis of the customer structure had shown that many new young customers were not retained: some of them left the bank again between the ages of 18 and 21 when their accounts began to incur costs.[18] For this reason the Marketing Director decided that the employees' focus should no longer be on the acquisition of new young customers, but on the targeted transition from a cost-free youth account to a cost-incurring private account.[19]

Below is an overview of the target groups and their activities:

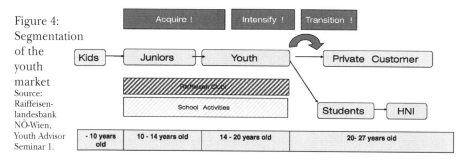

Figure 4: Segmentation of the youth market
Source: Raiffeisenlandesbank NÖ-Wien, Youth Advisor Seminar 1.

---

17 Cf. Interview 1, p 2.
18 See Chapter 2.3.
19 Cf. Marketing Director's journal entry of 20 May 2008.

For the Marketing Director this strategic realignment was accompanied by a change in the previous communication concept: in addition to existing short-term activities such as the acquisition of new accounts, she emphasized mid-term and long-term measures. In this context it was necessary above all to work together with schools.

The Marketing Director's aim was as follows:

"... I would like as a first step to expand our cooperation with schools. This makes sense in the long term because in this way we can reach many young people, even if it means a lot more work in the short term." [20]

A further important step for the Managing Director was then to concentrate on the predetermined goals for 2009.[21] Management's target for the year 2009 was the acquisition of 300 new youth accounts, which represented a 20% increase over the previous year. In view of the fact that the Marketing Department had just taken over responsibility for the area, it was very important for them to reach this predetermined acquisition target.

The Marketing Director and Team Leader worked together to set up a sales plan for 2009 in which measures for reaching the targets and the time schedule were determined. The emphases were no longer short-term activities, but were focused on longevity and sustainability, for example:

- The consolidation of existing customer relations, in order to make the transition from a free youth account to a cost-incurring private account easier.
- Sponsoring, in order to establish a good basis for long-term cooperation with schools in the area.

The Marketing Director was aware of the demands of communication and cooperation with the Team Leader and employees in order to reach the goals. The commitment of the employees played a central role in the implementation of these activities and in the sales approach. In accordance with the concept of the learning organization, she invested in the team as a system.[22]

---

20 Cf. Marketing Director's journal entry of 20 May 2008.
21 Cf. Marketing Director's journal entry of 4 November 2008.
22 Cf. Marketing Director's journal entry of 29 October 2008.

5 The Marketing Director's concept of leadership – from hierarchy to team

Until November 2008 the meetings of the youth advisors were hierarchically organized. The Team Leader described them as follows:

"The Club meetings were tightly organized and left absolutely no room for discussion. Contributions by the youth advisors (employees, note: Astrid Valek) were not scheduled."[23]

In future the employees were to contribute to the team and form it. To signal the new start, the Marketing Director convened a workshop, which took place on 9 December 2008 with the motto "Together to Success". The Marketing Director presented the sales plan and targets for 2009. She confirmed her trust and placed her hope in the strength of the individual employees and the team.

First ideas and wishes for the future were ascertained. The Marketing Director agreed to consider these concerns when planning. This agreement resulted first in astonishment, and later in the process, in gratification, which led to lively discussion about their collective future. There were many, partly uncoordinated, requests to speak and an abundance of ideas. Out of this, the need for more co-determination and co-design in terms of the complexity of customer demands and individual motivation crystallized on the meta-level:

"I wish that campaigns weren't centrally rolled out any longer, but could be attuned to my customers' needs."[24]

"I wanted to be a designer and not just carry things out."[25]

The Marketing Director could emotionally and cognitively sense the strong commitment and the zest for action in all participants and was able to connect this with the concept of the learning organization: the group had a common vision of the future towards which they worked together.

6 Visionary move into the future and setback revealed in figures

The co-determination and co-design resulted in increased personal commitment on the part of the employees; their ideas and suggestions for this common future were transferred into daily business practice. Their integration

---

23 Interview 2, p. 1.
24 Interview 3, p. 1.
25 Interview 4, p. 1.

into the campaigns involved a great deal of extra work, since the special needs of the youth market had to be considered, which at that time resulted in increased complexity.

The feeling that they were departing on a new venture increased in the team in the following weeks. Their high degree of consensus and the campaigns, which had already begun, clarified their common vision of the future – THE vision.

Despite many time-consuming activities and the increased workload, the figures at the end of the first quarter of 2009 were not satisfactory. In the months of January, February and March a continuous increase in the opening of new accounts was in fact observed, but the predetermined goal was not reached. With target achievement of 16.33% rather than the planned 25%, the results were below target.

"...I had expected a different, much better result. Despite our many activities, we were not on target,"[26] said the Marketing Director, at that time disappointed in her expectations.

7 Delegate leadership to encourage learning about leadership

In the meantime the Marketing Director herself had developed and recognized that it made no sense to manage the area directly. This insight led her to the next important step: changing its organizational structure. The change previously put in place had already affected the area very positively. The Marketing Director had succeeded in withdrawing from daily business in order to gain time for dealing with strategic and conceptual marketing tasks. She took a step back, delegating leadership and thus learning.

On 7 April 2009 she named her employee with many years of experience as Assistant Team Leader. At 24, this employee was at the same age as the target group, had shown great interest in the area during the preceding months and took over with great commitment.[27]

"I value the work with youth very much. It allows me a great deal of creativity in my daily work. Working documents can be individually adapted. I also look forward to having my own independent field of responsibility in which there is reciprocal motivation without competition,"[28] said the Assistant Team Leader.

---

26 Cf. Marketing Director's journal entry of 4 April 2009.
27 Cf. Marketing Director's journal entry of 7 April 2009.
28 Interview 5, p. 1.

From that point the Marketing Director began dealing only with the strategic steering of the area. When necessary she supported and counseled from the sidelines. Daily business was taken care of independently by the two Team Leaders.[29]

8 Encouraging team learning through a positive perspective

The change of organizational structure was announced at the Youth Club meeting on 16 April 2009, at which the results of the first quarter were also presented and discussed. The Marketing Director and the Team Leaders all deliberately spoke only about the positive signals and the continuous monthly growth. All three of them avoided negative statements and assigning blame for the failure to meet the target, because the team was doing good work. The Marketing Director was confident that the common goal of 300 new accounts by year's end could be achieved.[30] Strong personal mastery and the will to reach the desired goal could be clearly felt in all three managers.

To generate visible success and to focus the group's energies, the team developed a marketing activity. The youth advisor from the Maria Lanzendorf branch suggested that certificates be distributed in school classes, congratulating the pupils on their good grades and offering a youth banking account with a starting balance of € 20 or an MP3 player. All those in attendance approved. Nineteen of twenty-five schools in the region agreed to participate in the promotion.[31] This was a first visible success resulting from the previous cooperation with the schools. The idea of the certificates was correspondingly marketed and implemented when the school year ended at the beginning of July. The campaign was successful; many new accounts were opened. The numbers for the second quarter of 2009 were good and nearly on target.

9 The team's long-term success in the context of the organization

The certificate campaign was not a one-time success; rather, continuity began to appear in the handling of the market. The other activities in the sales

---

29 Cf. Duties and Responsibilites of Marketing Employees 2009.
30 Cf. Marketing Director's journal entry of 16 April 2009.
31 Cf. Interview 3, p. 1.

plan also developed well. No one had reckoned with such good results: by the end of July some of the branches had already either achieved or were within reach of their year-end goals.

The handling of the market took on a completely new dynamic among the employees. Rivalry began among the areas as to where more new accounts could be opened. The marketing management appreciated the team for its good work; success was celebrated.[32]

The results at the end of the third quarter were well above target, since the months after the special campaign had also gone very well. Eight out of twelve branches either reached or exceeded their targets. The management congratulated the team and promised to reward their commitment with a year-end bonus.[33]

Individual success *and* team success: in one branch the youth advisor had been on an advanced training course for two months, which caused their results to lag behind target. Therefore, at the Youth Club meeting on 13 October 2009, the other youth advisors offered their colleague their help and support. This was remarkable and had never happened before.[34]

It was also remarkable that the personnel situation among the youth advisors was stable for the first time in a long time. To be a youth advisor had achieved greater significance in the bank. The youth advisor from the Himberg branch said:

"The work with youth is highly significant for me. The youth market is very important for the bank and thus for me as well. The work is appreciated now and we are also rewarded."[35]

As of 31 December 2009, 455 new youth accounts had been opened and a majority of the youth accounts had been transformed into cost-incurring private accounts. All in all, the set target of 300 new accounts had been not only achieved but also exceeded by far.

Although the target had been reached, the team continued to work with just as much commitment all the way to the end of the year. For the Marketing Director this underscored the assumption of the learning organization that motivation and learning are closely linked. When, as in this case, management succeeds in creating a successful framework, the basis has been laid for individual and collective learning.

---

32 Cf. Marketing Director's journal entry of 13 October 2009.
33 Interview 1, p. 2.
34 Cf. Marketing Director's journal entry of 13 October 2009.
35 Interview 6, p. 1.

10 Conducive and protective management attitudes

The Marketing Director was aware that applying the concept of the learning organization can cause irritation in the beginning, most especially in people who for decades have been used to traditional leadership, because what an employee expects is not what happens. When employees are involved in decisions and collective reflection is permitted, this can be construed as a weakness in leadership. In the case of the Raiffeisenbank Region Schwechat this did not happen because the team of youth advisors was very young and ready to tread new paths.

Neither the management nor outsiders were able to determine the reasons for this success because it was very difficult to substantiate the causes. In the example of the Raiffeisenbank Region Schwechat the only proof was the positive development and the good results in the area. The management attributed the success to various circumstances, for example the good teamwork between marketing and youth advisors.

The Marketing Director had created the framework within which her team was able to advance. This did not cause much of a stir and played out in the background. Therefore what she did was recognized and appreciated by the team of youth advisors but not to the same degree by her superiors. This was due to the fact that the model of the learning organization was only applied in one department rather than in the entire organization. One person acted differently than the others, and as is usually the case in traditional companies, had to call attention to her successes and sell them. One example of the difficulty of receiving recognition was the salary negotiations with management during which the Marketing Director had to emphasize her deserts with all her powers of persuasion.

For one department in a hierarchically led company to succeed in establishing a completely different culture can be attributed to the facts that the Marketing Director acted to protect the learning and that no outsider observed in detail how the people in the department were acting. Thus there was no disruptive intervention from outside. This permitted the tolerance, which was necessary for learning to grow in a protected space. The only thing, which counted for management was the area's good results.

11 Possible scenarios

11.1 Expanding organizational learning

What happens when organizational learning expands?

Here the assumption is that any learning unit can transfer learning to others. The greatest effects would probably be expected in Sales, meaning the seventy employees who are responsible for handling the strategic business areas private customers, business customers and private banking.

In each case there is a leader who determines what is to be done and basically makes key decisions alone. In expanding organizational learning the example of the youth market could serve as best practice. Managers are catalysts and sponsors of the collective learning process. It should be noted here that precisely in recent times there have been tendencies for younger employees to demand greater rights to co-determination and as a result to be included more. Various meetings, such as branch manager meetings or daily team meetings, are used for reflection. One small step in the direction of the learning organization has already been taken; a further one is totally conceivable. Great leverage in the first step was probably provided by the will of the company management and the managers to establish a learning organization.

In order for the model to become viable, in the first instance the attitudes of management must change: when it has become self-evident that managers create frameworks so that their employees can learn and develop, innovative teams will come into being, and not before. Employees will talk with each other, exchange knowledge and experience, perceive contradictions and use them as opportunities for further development. Contact with each other, commitment and teamwork between departments can create waves in the entire organization and transfer themselves to the surroundings. The consequences of the expansion of organization learning could be an increase in sales results and an accompanied strengthening of the Raiffeisenbank Region Schwechat's market position.

11.2 Power, not learning is at the forefront

How could organizational learning be lost again?

A new manager takes over the youth market area and orients himself towards the bank's usual traditional management style. This person relies on known patterns and the desire for power and control outweighs everything else: the management style would be more hierarchical, the team of youth advisors would no longer be seen as representing the interests and perspectives of the customers. Since the youth advisors no longer actively co-design and contribute, there is also no common search for solutions and no more reflection as a team. Motivation and commitment among the youth advisors sink drastically. They do what is demanded of them but no longer actively give of themselves. They identify less with their areas of responsibility. Management misses out on important feedback and input from its team. One can only speculate on the impact and results.

Since the new manager is under pressure to make his mark and has to create visible success, short-term thinking in the sense of quick wins will predominate. The manager's own interests will outweigh those of others; team members will no longer exchange knowledge and experience, but use them in their own interests – therefore these can no longer be used productively. Mistakes will be covered up rather than being used as opportunities for learning.

12 Summary of insights

In summary it can be recognized that there was already a basis for a learning organization at the Raiffeisenbank Region Schwechat in 2006, when management commissioned market research into the causes for the stagnation in turnover and assumed that urgency and a need for action existed. The coincidence of the organization's readiness and the Marketing Director's belief in the concept of the learning organization was crucial to her decision when she took over to steer a new course and apply the concept in her department.

The Raiffeisenbank Region Schwechat is predominantly hierarchically managed: the overall picture is of management giving clear instructions so that the employees work toward a predetermined goal. The Marketing Director implemented a new leadership culture in her team, which was permitted by the organization and management. The opinions, interests and ideas of the employees were considered when decisions were made.

The delegation of leadership had an impact on the behavior of both Team Leaders. After the Marketing Director withdrew from daily business they were even more committed than before. This can be explained by the fact that in the short term a vacuum was created which gave both Team Leaders the opportunities to learn and develop. They took over responsibility and leadership; this was accompanied by even greater commitment on their part.

The mutual visionary and operative leap into the future increased each individual's motivation and, at the same time, brought the team together. One prerequisite was risk readiness in the form of trust on the part of the Marketing Director. She relied on their abilities, making it possible for both individual and team learning potential to open up. Laying blame was discouraged and the team's energies were focused; in addition, the common vision yielded strength and drive. The mutual goal stood at the forefront at all times.

Success was not achieved immediately; rather it was the result of a long learning process, which was not always simple and during which each step was planned. The consequences of each step led to the next step. This also applies to the team, which learned to trust its own strength and to work together toward a goal.

The helpfulness, which resulted showed how much the team had grown together and how the common vision changed the group's perceptions: the target achievement of the individual branches was no longer at the forefront, but rather the overall goal of the business area. Systems thinking – the integration of all goals into one single comprehensive goal – had taken place.

The Marketing Director herself had also worked her way through an enormous development process – a clear delineation of the areas of responsibility between the Team Leaders and support by the manager for their leadership.

During the case the position of the Marketing Director changed decisively: originally she was the catalyst, but during the learning process she became her team's advisor and companion and then a coach to the Team Leaders and context designer for leadership. From being a lone warrior, she developed into the shaper of a common future and designer of a leadership culture.

The case shows that intensively steered communication processes are necessary. These are the core element of management work and require a different type of manager: in order to reach a team result which is more than the sum of the combined employees, companions are required who make sure that the abilities of every individual can meaningfully unfold in the complete context. Motivation, euphoria, enjoyment of the work and loyalty must all be encouraged. Only in this way can an atmosphere arise in which the goals of the company become the personal concerns of each employee. The right spirit in the company is decisive for success and an advance in the market, because it creates the added value for the customer, which in the end is what it is all about.

List of figures

Figure 1: Time bar 2006-2009.
Figure 2: Structural comparison by age: Active customers with an account 2003-2007.
Figure 3: New structure in the youth market area.
Figure 4: Segmentation of the youth market.

Index of sources and references

Empirical sources

Interview 1: Company Management, 2010.
Interview 2: Team Leader of the Youth Club, 2010.
Interview 3: Youth Advisor Schwadorf, 2010.
Interview 4: Youth Advisor Götzendorf, 2010.
Interview 5: Assistant Team Leader of the Youth Club, 2010.
Interview 6: Youth Advisor Himberg, 2010.

Raiffeisenlandesbank NÖ-Wien: Market research. Population development 2001-2006, 2007.

Raiffeisenbank Region Schwechat: Duties and Responsibilities of the Market Director and Team Leader. NWM, 2009.

Raiffeisenbank Region Schwechat: Analysis Controlling: Development of the Number of Active Customers, 2006.

Raiffeisenbank Region Schwechat: Analysis Controlling: Development of the Number of Customers by Age Group, 2009.

Raiffeisenbank Region Schwechat: Analysis Controlling: Development of the Number of Customers Private Customers, Business Customers and Private Banking, 2009.

Raiffeisenbank Region Schwechat: Annual Statement of Accounts of the RB Schwechat of 31.12.2006.

Raiffeisenbank Region Schwechat: Organizational Structure – Structural Organization of the RB Schwechat as of 30.11.2007.

Raiffeisenbank Region Schwechat: Website www.rbschwechat.at/überuns, Download: 22.4.2010.

Marketing Director's Journal, 2008.

References

Sattelberger, Thomas (Ed.) (1994), Die lernende Organisation. Konzepte für eine neue Qualität der Unternehmensentwicklung, 2nd edition. Gabler Verlag, Wiesbaden.

Senge, Peter (2008), Die fünfte Disziplin. Kunst und Praxis der lernenden Organisation, 5th edition. Klett-Cotta, Stuttgart.

Eva Maria Bauer . Andrea Berger[1]

Change while the engine is running – management challenges during an extensive change process in the public health sector

1 Introduction

This case presents a successful example, which clearly shows that courage to participate in a complex change process in the public sector on the part of those who are significantly involved leads to success. At its center is the consolidation of a number of European clinics[2] between 2004 and 2009 under the direction and management of a holding company. The goal was to establish a uniform organisational and communication structure between the holding company and the clinics.

Here, organisational development refers to the organisation as a whole. Organisational changes originating from the central holding company are examined. The restructuring, which took place within the individual clinics, is not considered; rather only the area of management development is explored.[3]

The result of the extensive process is that the central holding company no longer assigns tasks to the clinics or communicates directives; instead, it is slowly becoming a strategic partner. From 2004 to 2009 a number of organisational changes were necessary. The corporate group structure had consequences especially for managers, both in the central holding company and in the clinics; this created new challenges for them.

The results show that the main problems in creating a new clinic structure lie in finding vision and strategy, in securing the necessary flow of communication and in professional change management, and that during the integration the characteristics and histories of the individual facilities must be considered.

---

1 Andrea Berger wrote the Master's thesis; Eva Maria Bauer dealt further with the paper in an article.
2 Names of both the organisation and the people involved have been changed.
3 "Managers in the holding company" refers to department managers in the holding company. "Managers in the clinics" refers to management colleagues, i.e. the medical, sales and nursing care directors.

2 Initial situation

Initially there were more than twenty clinics, which in the course of four years were consolidated under one legal owner whose corporate management was taken over by a holding company.

2.1 The consolidation of various clinics as a learning opportunity for managers

Since 2008 the aforesaid clinics in Europe have employed around 19,000 workers. The holding company has more than 8,200 beds in over twenty facilities at its disposal. A total of 3,000 doctors and about 9,900 members of the nursing staff work there. Annually 167,000 operations are carried out and altogether there are more than 385,000 in-patients.[4]

The clinic holding company as a corporate body under public law has been in existence since July 2004. Its tasks include the operational management of the clinics, professional management based on medical and commercial criteria and the offer of health care services. Its goal is to ensure home-like patient care 365 days a year and to offer health care of the highest quality.[5]

2.2 Legal basis of the organisation

Due to the consolidation of the clinics under one owner and operational management, the need to decouple the operational management from the supervisory authority was recognised. The personnel resources and relevant data, which were necessary for the management and financing of the clinics remained in the clinic holding company; therefore that side of the ownership was tasked with establishing a clinic holding company. The process was conducted with the assistance of an external consultant.[6]

According to an amendment by a political decision-making unit enacted on 29 April 2004, the goals of the clinic holding company are the management and operation of the clinics, taking into consideration the basic principles of diligent commercial management and the obtaining of optimal

---

4 Cf. Website of the clinic holding company, downloaded on 28 February 2010.
5 Cf. Image brochure of the clinic holding company dated 2009.
6 Interview 3 (Managing Director), p. 9.

operating results.[7] At that time the imminent steps for implementation included the topics of personnel, finance, organisation and public relations.

The newly created organisation had to accomplish the following tasks:[8]
- Management and operation of all the clinics
- Maintenance of modern medical standards and optimal care for all patients in the clinics
- Conclusion of all contracts necessary for the operating procedures in the clinics, insofar as this did not affect the tasks of the legal owners
- Corporate supervision and operational management of a number of clinics

One country became legal owner of over twenty European clinics and the employment status of the employees of the clinics was also maintained.[9]

3 The consolidation of over twenty clinics into one large health services group

3.1 The structure of the clinic holding company in 2004

In 2004 two Managing Directors (MD Department 1, MD Department 2) shared the overall management of the clinic holding company. The administrative departments Strategy/Organisational Development, Legal, and Infrastructure Department reported directly to them. The administrative departments had no direct access to the clinics (e.g. they could not give direct instructions); rather they carried out the instructions of the Managing Directors.

The Finance, Controlling, Medical, Technology and Personnel Departments were tasked with the direct management of the clinics. The business of the holding company, in the sense of overall management, was run by the Managing Directors. It was the duty of each Managing Director continually to inform and consult with the other about important business transactions and matters which involved a number of business areas or which were of great importance.[10]

---

7   Cf. Minutes of the 50th standing committee meeting on 2 July 2004, p. 1 ff.
8   Cf. Minutes of the constitutive meeting in April 2004.
9   Cf. Informational e-mail from the managing directors to the department managers in the clinic holding company in August 2004.
10 Cf. §4 of the Internal Rules of Procedure of the clinic holding company, p. 3.

3.2 2004 – Learning from challenges

3.2.1 Changing management structures step by step

The establishment of the organisation in mid-2004 and the organisational changes it entailed were a difficult process, since at that time neither the management of the holding company nor the management of the clinics understood the new structures and the allocation of duties, which were involved.

"(...) Yes, it was really difficult to get a grip on that process. At the start there were so-called management meetings, but they dealt with almost nothing but finances. We passed directives on to the clinics. The mood, well, it was correspondingly bad. The directors in the clinics thought, super, now we've done all the work and so far we've done it very well, and then comes this holding company and tells us how to do our jobs." [11]

The representatives of the holding company and also those of the clinics were aware that the changes were very difficult for everyone who was involved in and had to carry out the change process.

3.2.2 Changing communication step by step

The clinic holding company was faced with the challenge of communicating to the clinics both the new structures and the imminent far-reaching changes. The difficulty was that the lines of authority in the holding company were not comprehensible, that is, in what form and who should communicate the structural changes. The management of the holding company would have liked uniform lines of communication to accompany the changes. The clinic's representatives, on the other hand, found that communication was sufficient.

"(...) There was very little communication with the clinics because it was not clear who should approach them." [12]

"(...) Much too little, one would have needed much more understanding in the clinics. There were individual initiatives but no one had the authority to make contact with the clinics where they were. There was too little internal communication; there was neither goal-oriented change management nor transparent organisational development." [13]

---

11 Interview 1 (Department Manager), p. 2.
12 Interview 3 (Managing Director), p. 10.
13 Interview 4 (Department Manager), p. 15.

"(...) In general the information was sufficient for me. When information or conditions were unclear I took it upon myself to ask. To me it was always important to have sufficient room to manoeuvre and creative leeway in my facility, and in that we were mostly successful."[14]

It can be seen that, due to the extensive changes, there would have been potential for more and clearer internal communication in order to explain to the personnel why the changes had become necessary, what structure the organisation would have in future, who their future contact partners would be and where authority and responsibility lay.

3.2.3 The uncertainty factor in the change process

The management of the holding company and the managers of the clinics were to communicate the changes; but without a precise description of their own authority, a vision, strategies or goals, this led to uncertainty on the part of all concerned.

"(...) We unfortunately had neither a vision nor concrete goals, only a to-do list which we had worked out together with the consultant. This consisted only of how operational synergies could be created and which aimed to get as much data as possible to the central office."[15]

"(...) There was no real vision; information was passed to the staff in the clinics orally, in written form or through press releases."[16]

At all levels a vision was missing. In 2004 data from the clinics was requested and information was then passed from the central holding company to the clinics. The structural changes became more complex. Clear lines leading toward management or cooperation between the holding company and the clinics could only be vaguely recognised; nevertheless efforts were made to communicate with the help of various channels. The goal of cost-cutting was still a major focus; the understanding of management in the newly founded organisation was not precisely defined and was therefore difficult to communicate.

---

14 Interview 6 (Director), p. 21.
15 Interview 1 (Department Manager), p. 3.
16 Interview 5 (Director), p. 18.

3.3 2005 – the turning point – first successes in the implementation

3.3.1 Adapting the structures: the first fruits are harvested

Around July 2005, on the initiative of the managers from three organisational areas, clearly defined scopes of duty were established. From this point in time a fund was responsible for strategic-political needs; the operational management of all clinics was the responsibility of the holding company.[17]

3.3.2. The tide turns – the structural changes are perceived more and more positively

The structural changes in July 2005 were rated positively by all interviewees (both those from the management of the holding company and those from the management of the clinics):

"(…) With immediate effect, the direct contact person was the Regional Manager. Thus a rapid flow of information and operationalized target setting became possible."[18]

"(…) It was the beginning of management structures for the management of a group."[19]

These statements clearly show that clarity of management structures and allocation of duties were important for successful cooperation between the central office and the individual facilities.

These are the facts: The rules of the game for cooperation between the holding company and the fund were set by the owner and the management, as a consequence all official communication from the fund to the clinics had to take place via the holding company. Where quality control and on-site inspections were involved, parallel information was sent to the Regional Manager involved.[20]

---

17 Cf. Employee Magazine Issue 1/05, p. 4.
18 Interview 5 (Director), p. 18.
19 Interview 6 (Director), p. 22.
20 Cf. Strategy paper management consultancy dated 28 May 2005, p. 10.

3.3.3 The changes bear their first fruits
The regional management further reduces the complexity of the organisation

In the newly structured holding company there were three management areas plus regional management. From that time the five Regional Managers were responsible for the operative management of the clinics and the establishment of strategic projects and medical optimisation in the region. Direct financial responsibility for the conduct of the clinics, the operative management of the individual clinics and regional medical care rested with the regional management.[21] In the middle of 2005 the central holding company was divided into three management areas (medical, commercial and personnel). These were supported by the service units, central functions and administrative departments. Where regional management was concerned, direct responsibility for management and results as well as the organisation of management structures rested with the clinics.

3.3.4 The introduction of regional management has a positive impact

The management and the Department Managers in the central holding company saw advantages in the introduction of regional management:
 "(…) The Regional Managers are not only responsible for operative implementation but are also involved in the development of strategy. (…) Regional Managers must be good communicators, must pass on information, clarify tasks to the clinics, and lead purposefully. They must implement the directives in the clinics."[22]

Through the regional concept, the central holding company can more intensively realise its strategic tasks, while the Regional Managers work directly together with the Department Managers in the clinics in their respective regions, communicating information on-site and developing implementation concepts together.

In the area of personnel development, seminar organisation was standardised in the central holding company, and the compilation of a training concept was begun to determine standard procedures for training and continuing education with reference to target groups, conditions and countries. Further, the compilation of a training catalogue was initiated; this was to

---

21 Cf. Employee Magazine Issue 1/05, p. 4
22 Interview 4 (Department Manager), p. 14.

include all offers of specialist and personal development in the areas of patient care and administration.[23]

In 2005 management structures were developed which reduced the management distance between the central holding company and the clinics. With the support of the regional managers, the central holding company's requirements could be realized. On the other hand, however, individual measures could also be implemented to involve employees in the development process. This helped to develop the organisation and the people working for it together and to lead them to a new mutual identity.

3.4 2006: Growing and struggling toward a mutual identity – the Personnel Department introduces measures

One of the change projects initiated by the clinic holding company was intended to ensure a mutual overall concept, a common catalogue of norms and values, as well as the realisation of the strategic goals of the clinic holding company.[24]

In that year the executive management and owner tasked the Personnel Department with the development of a mutual understanding of vision, mission, values and basic principles. In 2006 the steering committee, consisting of executive management, Regional Managers, the works council of the central holding company and representatives of all professional groups, began to work on the central guiding ideas and objectives. The goal was the development and realisation of a mutual vision of modern health care centers to be held and lived by all employees.[25]

For the first time ever, an educational programme for the entire organisation was developed. This included a broad spectrum of personal development support with communication at its center.[26] In seminars for and across professional groups, subjects such as communication, project management and corporate management were covered. Facilities were offered in which training and further education courses related to specific fields could be attended.[27]

---

23 Cf. Progress report 2005
24 Cf. Progress report 2005.
25 Cf. Progress report 2005.
26 Cf. Progress report 2005.
27 Cf. Progress report 2005.

3.4.1 The implementation in detail

The first steps on the path to a mutual training concept were viewed as almost totally problematic, because they began with a training concept for all workers and at the start the education of managers received hardly any attention.

"(...) I am of the opinion that first the managers should have been prepared for the new structures and given the tools to find their way around the new structures in the new group and also to pass this on suitably to the employees." [28]

"(...) It didn't work all that well. With the creation of the education programme they simply zeroed in on one star in the heavens. It was nothing but a marketing and PR instrument. At that time there was not yet any strategic personnel development. The measures were not directed toward the targets and requirements of the organisation. The goals and strategies were never described." [29]

The educational programme was, however, seen as a basically sensible measure by the interviewees, but this was not a part of strategic personnel management: since according to their statements this did not exist at the time, further education measures could not be embedded in it. On the one hand the central holding company continually started initiatives to school the employees and give them the possibility to develop themselves. On the other hand the managers in the clinics were not prepared for the new management challenges in the group.

3.5 2007: The beginning of a general orientation project

At the beginning of January 2007 an extensive general orientation project was begun. Its goal was to allow the approximately 15,000 employees at that time to formulate their own mutual ideals for their day-to-day working life and to challenge them to take their professional future into their own hands. The intent was that it would become clear that the individuality of the respective clinics should be maintained but that changes and restructuring were necessary for the clinics due to the network of the holding company.[30]

Over 1,000 employees were actively involved in creating the mutual overall concept.[31] In the workshops the participants exchanged experiences of

---

28 Interview 1 (Department Manager), p. 4.
29 Interview 4 (Department Manager), p. 14 f.
30 Cf. Employee Magazine Issue 3/07, p. 4.
31 Employee Magazine Issue 02/06.

the professional day-to-day lives and thus were able to find new ways together to cooperate.

In the overall concept, in connection with the topic of management, it was determined that the individual clinics should cooperate intensively in order to achieve the greatest possible synergy effects.

As can be seen from the overall concept, for the clinic holding company management means creating framework conditions which enable employees to fulfil their tasks independently and efficiently, to motivate them through appreciation and thus to enable them to succeed. In addition, importance was attached to supporting the employees individually in their professional development.[32]

In June 2007 the 81 representatives of the clinics, in the presence of the Department Managers, presented the future basis for cooperation for the more than 15,000 employees. The overall concept they created is the result of the extensive general orientation project.

The next step was to work together to take the overall concept in the form of presentations to the clinics.[33] Since every clinic had its own structures, processes, priorities and thus approaches, individual implementation measures were planned. In order (also) to anchor the general concept institutionally, plans were made for a permanent committee, e.g. a board or group with advisory and coordinating functions in each clinic.[34] These measures, involving the employees, were steps towards a mutual development of the organisation and the creation of a mutual corporate identity.

3.5.1 The realisation of the overall concept

The commitment of the employees in the general orientation process was rated positively by all the interviewees; the design of the process in and for itself was critically questioned.

"(...) The general orientation process was in and of itself a good thing, but in the end it was primarily a marketing gag. The process had definitely consumed too many resources. But without a vision the overall concept cannot be brought to life. I think the general orientation process was only good for the people who were involved. For a long time the people in the clinics did not know what the holding company does, despite the overall concept."[35]

---

32 Website of the clinic holding company, accessed on 13 March 2010.
33 Cf. Employee Magazine Issue 3/07, p. 6.
    Cf. Employee Magazine Issue 2/05, p. 4.
35 Interview 1 (Department Manager), p.4.

"(...) A really good idea, but from my point of view far too soon. We would first have needed visions and goals; then we could have started with the overall concept. A few of my employees were intensively involved with the development of the overall concept. They were very committed, but unfortunately it was not possible to impart this enthusiasm for a mutual identity to the employees in our clinic – because there were no mutual vision and no mutual goals." [36]

"(...) It was extremely important, and it was also right to start the process. But they started it without leadership, without organisational goals, without strategy. The overall concept was worked out by employees of all levels, but they all had different perceptions of the organisation, different values and goals. The result was only a compromise, not a consensus." [37]

Although the general orientation process was viewed positively, there were points of criticism, such as the lack of goals, visions and corporate values, the overly early start of the process, the enormous investment of personnel resources and the lack of proper transmission of the results to the employees. At this point in the process consciousness was raised that the development of an overall concept needs clear goals, visions and corporate values as well as adjudicated responsibilities at all management levels, in order to be able to act efficiently in relation to both personnel and costs. Here communication difficulties were also the logical consequence of transmitting and anchoring the overall concept.

3.6 2008: Management structures gain importance

The clinic holding company became one of the largest public health care services in Europe.

3.6.1 New demands on managers bring change in turn

Due to the group structure and the very rapid growth of the organisation, the management requirement profile changed. It was no longer sufficient to be a good specialist and come to terms with the daily administration; social competences and control of resources were in demand.[38] These changes were perceived differently in the holding company and the clinics.

---

36 Interview 2 (Director), p. 7.
37 Interview 4 (Department Manager), p. 15.
38 Cf. Modified Management Requirement Profile.

The new group structure brought along changes for the individual managers in the clinics. They were challenged to implement requirements together with their respective Regional Managers and in cooperation with other clinics in their regions.

"(...) For me it has become more difficult and challenging. Now I am much more a manager. I must be there for my employees, but also report to the regional management or to the central office. Overall I have more management tasks within the group."[39]

The managers in the clinics who were polled primarily saw new contact partners, more management tasks and greater corporate thinking and action in the new group structure.

"(...) The managers have to communicate downwards as well as possible, that is, to their employees; that hasn't changed. Often, however, it was the case that the Department Managers didn't manage, but only administrated. The group requires a new aspect: a new understanding of management per se, but the changes in the group structure also have to be communicated. And that requires management. The managers have to motivate their employees and show them that changes are also opportunities. In addition, managers also need increased responsibility for processes; that isn't about responsibility for results or one's area. They have to take care that things happen and that the result is right in the end."[40]

A new management structure, as can be seen from the interviews, brings new challenges for every employee in a management position. To cope with this, a new project was started.

3.6.2 Further education for managers and a mutual management culture as a factor for success

The owner and executive management initiated a steering group for a management development programme, consisting of the three Managing Directors, two employees from the Personnel Department, two Regional Managers, a Medical Director, a Nursing Services Director and a Commercial Director. A quarterly employee magazine accompanied the entire project. This steering group developed a concept for management development on the basis of interviews with managers in the clinics and online questionnaires.

The analysis showed, for example, that the difference between specialist and management tasks for the managers might be very small. There were

---

39 Interview 2 (Director), p. 7.
40 Interview 4 (Department Manager), p. 15.

evidently deficits in the transparency of the organisational processes between the individual clinics and regional management and also between the Departmental Managers, Regional Managers and the central holding company. The managers saw sufficient room to manoeuver for their own strategies in each medical institution and evaluated the communication within the medical institutions as affective and emotional.

The management training stages were divided into three modules: business management, self-management and leadership, and ranged from strategic environmental analysis through conflict resolution to deployment and supervision of teams.[41]

3.6.3 The training modules for managers

In retrospect the training modules were very positively rated both by the Managing Directors and Department Managers in the holding company and by the managers in the clinics:

The seminars, которые were offered, communicated a management culture to the organisation and contributed to the establishment of a mutual understanding of management. It can also be seen, however, that it would have been important for these seminars to be held earlier; they would even have been needed right at the start of the change process.

"(...) Yes, they were great. The seminars should already have been offered in 2004. They conveyed to me the management culture in this organisation."[42]

"(...) The training modules were extremely important and very good; understanding of management was honed, so that all the managers in the group were on the same page. So everybody has the same understanding of what to do and when to lead. More measures are planned, such as a module called Management and Responsibility, Change Management with Planning and Implementation."[43]

"(...) That was absolutely interesting and on the one hand helped us all to get to know our colleagues in the other hospitals better. It also promoted the community, and we learned what the concept 'management' meant to the owner and what would be required of us as managers in future. I personally also learned a great deal for my daily work and for dealing with my employees."[44]

---

41 Cf. Management development programme of the clinic holding company, stand 5 February 2008, p. 10.
42 Interview 2 (Director), p. 7.
43 Interview 4 (Department Manager), p. 15.
44 Interview 5 (Director), p. 19.

The statements show that the seminars conveyed a new and mutual logic of management. They also contributed to helping the managers in the group to get to know each other better and promoted the acceptance of the professional groups among themselves.

A number of measures were initiated by the Managing Directors in the holding company for the clinics to improve the management structures in the organisation: the introduction of regional management, the initiation of the general orientation process and the management development programme.

3.7 2009: Organisational development in the central holding company is further optimised

In 2009 the central holding company was subdivided into two large business areas, each of which report to a Managing Director. The main task of the central departments established under these two business areas is the provision of services and strategies for more than twenty decentralised clinics. As part of a project with the goal of creating a positive new beginning in the holding company, the organisational structure was made leaner. In the commercial area the span of control was reduced and a more effective purchasing organisation was established. In the medical area a clear segregation of duties between the departments for Strategic Quality Development and for Medical and Nursing Care Operational Support was created.

3.7.1 The new principle of management and accountability logic

The Regional Managers are the hubs between the central holding company and the clinics in their regions. They contributed significantly to the strategic focusing of the organisation and were responsible for realisation of the central holding company's requirements together with the clinics in their regions.

The five Regional Managers were responsible for operative management in the regions. Organisationally, they reported to the Managing Director for Commerce. The Regional Managers were supported through coordinators in the areas of information technology and facility management. They were contact partners for the clinics in purchasing procedures or large projects such as the introduction of SAP. The central departments, each under the direction of a Managing Director, were responsible for the central provision of services and the development of strategies.

3.7.2 The changed management style between 2004 and 2009 is a trend-setter for the further development of the organisation

The role of the central holding company, and thus the management style as well, were fundamentally transformed between 2004 and 2009. The holding company and the clinics as well consider the change in management style as positive. More independence and creative leeway for the clinics were discernible; on the other hand the holding company was able to concentrate more on its strategic tasks. Through clear allocation of duties rapid improvement in cooperation, communication and the climate within the whole organisation occurred.

"(…) From mid-2005 to about mid-2008 there was a very centralised focus on the holding company, with a great deal of friction. The new structure is a modern group structure, a very lean group management, with advisers in the core business and a distinct service character in the commercial area. Responsibility for results – for the entire organisation assigned to the Managing Directors, of course – rests with the Regional Managers for the individual regions. Thus the Managing Directors can concentrate on strategic questions, while business operations rest primarily with the Regional Managers and the managers in the clinics."[45]

"(…) The central holding company sees itself as a service organisation for operative questions and is, however, also responsible for strategic issues. Campaigns are implemented with management systems. In the past the role of the holding company was not clear (…) now it is different: we work together with the Regional Managers and representatives of the clinics on directives, which are then communicated further to the clinics by the Regional Managers. The clinics were involved in the development of the directives; therefore these more quickly achieve greater acceptance than in the past."[46]

Through numerous structural changes and a new management culture it was possible to realign the entire organisation.

---

45 Interview 3 (Managing Director), p.11.
46 Interview 4 (Department Manager), p.16.

3.7.3 Subsequent reflection on the change process from the point of view of the managers

The interviewees had differing opinions on the planning of the change process. The palette ranged from strengthening the regions, establishing the central holding company from the beginning on as a strategic partner, and having visions and goals, all the way to integration and change management and the flow of information:

"(...) They should have done it differently right from the start, strengthening the regions and establishing the central holding company as a strategic partner. We needed to have a vision from the beginning. We passed the pressure from the owner one-to-one on to the clinics. At the start the central holding company signalled: 'Now we're coming to save you,' fears were not allayed but rather stirred up. The people involved were not made into people concerned. At the beginning there was no formulation of goals, authority was taken away from the clinics and at the start management was too authoritarian." [47]

"(...) First develop goals and visions and only then create a mutual identity. To be a reliable partner for the clinics right from the start – in my opinion that would have been the most important thing." [48]

"(...) The integration and change management. They should have helped the employees better to acclimatize themselves to the changed environment. We should have conveyed to them: Jump into the boat; we're going to travel with you to a mutual future." [49]

"(...) One interviewee stressed the importance of the information management to the employees, for example to fill a brochure with the contents of the current homepage and distribute it to the colleagues who were taken over." [50]

"(...) Another interviewee pointed out the necessity of more time for the implementation and consideration of the previous culture and history of the organisation. As I've already said in answer to one of the other questions, you had the impression: 'Now we're coming to show you how it works'. That created a lot of mistrust and lack of understanding among the managers. The managers in the clinics were not seen as proper partners." [51]

The employees in the clinics would have liked to be better prepared for the extensive change process and to feel that there was more understanding

---

47 Interview 1 (Department Manager), p. 5.
48 Interview 2 (Director), p. 8.
49 Interview 4 (Department Manager), p. 16.
50 Interview 5 (Director), p. 20.
51 Interview 6 (Director), p. 23.

for the previous organisational culture in the individual clinics. For the interviewees, the future of the organisation lay in continuing to convey to the employees where the added value of the complete organisation lay for them personally.[52] The holding company for the clinics should be a bottom-up organisation with clear responsibilities for the employees in the core business and competence centers in the central holding company.[53]

The lack of vision, lack of strategic focus, the insufficient internal information and communication flows, the unprofessional change management and the intense pressure from outside emerged as the greatest problems. Further, the role of the central holding company was not defined in detail. The managers in the clinics were not sufficiently prepared for the new requirements, did not know the tasks of the central holding company and did not know what would be expected of them in future. This led at the beginning to uncertainty across the entire group. If one looks at the big picture it becomes clear that learning can also take place in a very complex example such as the consolidation of clinics. So – despite initial difficulties and lack of vision and goals – they constantly worked on continuing the change process and integrating the employees on all levels. Ultimately the employees in the individual clinics found a new basis for a mutual future through the installation of new, regional organisational and management structures – taking into account the specialist and leadership skills of the managers in the clinics.

4 Scenarios for the future

A positive scenario presents the ideal case for the further development of the organisation. A negative scenario presents negative development which could come upon the organisation.

4.1 Positive scenario: "Competition grows, development is spurred"

The organisation's clinic holding company is about to master the following challenges:

- financial constraints

---

52 Interview 1 (Department Manager), p. 5.
53 Interview 3 (Managing Director), p. 12.

- affordable and sustainable assurance of health care provision and quality
- demographics: more and older patients, fewer premium payers, fewer beds
- developments in the labour market: employee qualifications, fewer employees (doctors, nursing attendants)

These changed framework conditions require new goals:
- assurance of the health care provision of the population of Lower Austria with hospital services and simultaneous adherence to available resources
- sustainable financial feasibility of health care through effective provision of services and utilisation of synergy potential in the network of 27 facilities under one roof
- high patient and employee satisfaction through contracted deployment of instruments at defined locations
- further image improvement among employees and the general population

The management of the holding company for the clinics began a long-term extensive organisational development process at the beginning of 2010.

In the process the following points were to be implemented:
- uniform performance by management and employees with a mutual commitment to the organisation's holding company for the clinic
- efficiency in the areas of quality and economy
- high satisfaction among patients and employees

A central factor for realisation of these goals is that every employee knows the added value of the future goals and his or her own contribution to those goals. Here knowledge of the superordinate goals and cooperation within the organisation are the most important criteria.

In the organisational development process a higher ceiling is built under which existing projects and measures are integrated, networked or supplemented. The success of this process is based on the central formula $S = Q \times A$ (success = quality x acceptance). Every employee should know what he or she in his or her job could contribute to the superordinate goals (department, hospital or region).

Communication is the central element of support in this organisational development process in order to improve the organisation's performance, reach the fixed business objectives and accompany the organisational development process. Responsibility rests with the managers to communicate the same message, speak the same language and walk the talk.

In the future the clinic holding company will concentrate on the following topics and fields of action: economy, patients, employees, communication and image.

> The following strategies will be followed:
> - In-patient admittance and length of in-patient stays as short as can be justified medically and with relation to caregiving. The relevant measurement indictors are: length of stay, re-admission rate, exhaustion of the out-patient clinic potential
> - Target-orientated patient-centred care (e.g. nursing home, permanent vegetative state, rehabilitation)
> - Patients must receive state of the art treatment, in the right place, at the right time, with optimal resources.
> - Implementation of the health care mandate and assurance of clinic-specific effectiveness (quality, economy) of the individual patient-care models

From this it follows that the concrete organisational goals must be communicated by the managers to the employees in order to assure that they are accepted and implemented. Ideally the organisational development process in the next two to three years will be successful and will contribute to the establishment of a common organisational culture and a mutual identity. This is the basis for all further positive development steps by the clinic holding company, for example needs-based training and continuing education for all professional groups in the consolidated clinics, incentive schemes for special achievements, new projects which are initiated bottom-up, open, transparent internal and external communication, clear management structures, further improvements in medical and nursing care, financial efficiency, cooperation and synergies among all of the clinics, above all within one area of responsibility of a regional management. The correct and sustainable control of the areas mentioned above makes the holding company for the clinics a large and extremely successful health care service provider with employees who are proud of their organisation, satisfied patients and an excellent image.

4.2 Negative scenario: "Loss of power for the central holding company, disintegration of the organisation"

If management is not successful in its attempts to further optimise management structures, consolidate the organisation and bring about constructive cooperation in medical, nursing and commercial aspects, there is the possibility that the individual clinics will drift apart. This could lead to a situation in which regional managers no longer work for the benefit of the organisation as a whole but follow their own interests or those of the individual clinics. Through the introduction of additional levels of management, there are no sufficiently clear responsibilities; this in return leads to dissatisfied employees.

> In summary, the organisation could experience negative development with regard to the following points:
> - redundancy in medical care
> - uncoordinated medical business activities within the regions
> - economic inefficiency
> - few innovations due to demotivated employees
> - dissatisfied patients and bad image

Due to a bad image it becomes difficult for the organisation to attract highly qualified employees in medicine and nursing or guarantee their long-term loyalty to the organisation. Redundancy in medical care provision may lead to long waiting times for operations and treatments, and thus to dissatisfied patients.

4.3 Recapitulation and reflection on the empirical insights

The first two years were challenging for those involved because neither a clear common vision nor a strategic focus nor transparent goals had been achieved. There was only the requirement that the existing clinics were to be integrated into a central holding company and – with the primary goal of cost reduction – be corporately managed. Under these conditions the clinic holding company could not coalesce, which made further changes necessary. At the beginning there was uncertainty and irritation among the employees in the clinics, although they were at no point in danger of losing their jobs. That was because the employees had worked for a long time in a very stable environment and were not used to dealing with change. The direct management of the clinics by the central holding company led to a management vacuum, which did not improve until 2005, when regional management was introduced.

In July 2005 first structural changes occured: the delinking of strategic tasks from operational management. In 2005 it went further – through the introduction of regional management – towards stronger regionalisation: management responsibility for the clinics in the respective regions rested with regional management. Through the Regional Managers, operationalized objectives and a rapid flow of information were enabled.

On the one hand the new structures involving regional management reduced the managers' workloads, decreased the scope of control and were a significant component of the management hierarchy of the holding company. On the other hand, the Regional Managers were not only responsible for operational implementation but also involved in strategic development. They needed to be good communicators, lead purposefully and implement the owner's requirements. The careful management by the regional managers was an important milestone in the coalescence of the organisation and enabled further positive development.

In 2007 a common overall concept was developed. Looking back, it was not possible to get this into the employee's heads with lasting effect, not least because of the lack of a common vision and strategy.

Not until 2008, when a systematic management development programme was introduced, it became possible to convey a new mutual understanding of management. Its goal was to prepare the managers for the new demands of their role. More than ever, social competence and resource allocation were needed. The managers now had more responsibility for processes, and the size of the organisation required extensive corporate and managerial thinking and action.

In 2009 a professional organisational development project was begun, with the goal of ensuring the efficient management of the clinics: the central departments, each under the leadership of one managing director, are responsible for the central provision of services and development of strategy. The five Regional Managers are responsible for operative management in their regions. Organisationally the Regional Managers report directly to the Managing Directors. After approval by regional management, directives are implemented by the employees in the clinics.

In summary, the conclusion can be drawn that in the beginning phase the employees were not very involved and the Department Managers in the clinics were deprived of their management authority. In 2007–2008 executive management began to re-delegate management tasks to the managers in the clinics and a new management philosophy was established across the whole organisation. These changes in structure were THE decisive factor, which allowed the employees and managers to coalesce into one common organisation.

Bibliography

Empirical sources

Department managers (2004). Minutes of the 50th standing committee meeting on 2nd July 2004.

Evaluation of questionnaires by the clinic holding company as part of the management development programme (14th May 2008).

Management development programme (concept paper) of the clinic holding company (5th February 2008).

Managing directors (2004). Informational e-mail from the managing directors to the department managers in the clinic holding company (2nd August 2004).

Employee magazine of the clinic holding company, Issues 1/05, 2/05, 3/07, 4/07, 2/08.

Image brochure of the clinic holding company (2009).

Interviews with managing directors and managers (March/April 2010).

Clinic holding company, internal presentation (5th February 2008).

Minutes of the 22nd meeting of the clinic holding company, Agenda Item 5 (24th May 2005).

Minutes of the employees' meeting (17th January 2008).

Paragraph 4 of the internal rules of procedure for the executive management.

Strategy paper management consultancy (28th May 2005).

Strategy paper management consultancy on the subject of organisational development (27th February 2009).

Progress report of the clinic holding company (2005).

Video of the general orientation project (July 2007).

Website of the clinic holding company (2008), downloaded on 28th February 2010.

Harald Gansfuss . Maria Spindler[1]

Merger as the motivation for the move from extended workbench to independent company

Using the example of NOVAK CZECH[2]

1 Introduction

The focus of these observations is NOVAK CZECH, a medium-sized Czech company, and its challenges and solutions deriving from the acquisition of a second company. The case study describes the steps taken as the company moved from being an extended workbench[3] of an Austrian family business towards independence. This metamorphosis did not always go according to plan; the parties developed solutions through both their actions and their failures. We will present the central measures of change from the purchase in 2003 through the first effects of the transformed leadership in 2006. The points of departure prior to 2003 are presented as preconditions dating as far back as 1992. The effects of the transformation are presented for the following four years, through 2010.

2 Initial situation[4]

2.1 Overview of the companies involved

In 2003 two companies existed separately and independently from each other. In the following graphic the seller group and buyer group are clearly separated.

---

1 Harald Gansfuss wrote the Master's thesis; Maria Spindler developed it further into this article, which was translated from the German by Deborah Starkey.
2 The names of the companies as well as those of the individual persons have been changed.
3 In this context, "extended workbench" is understood to mean a company which neither develops nor brings to market products of its own, but rather offers contract manufacture of products which are developed and sold by other companies.
4 The history and initial situation of the case in the period from 1992 through March 2003 are presented.

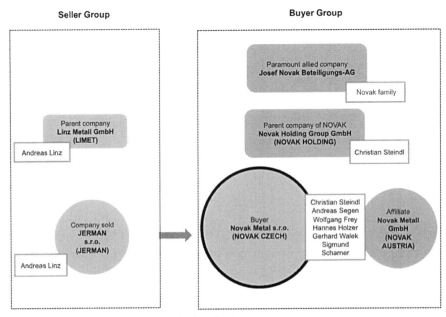

Figure 1: Overview of the companies involved

Both, the seller (Andreas Linz) and the buyers (the Novak family), were deeply interested in the successful consolidation of JERMAN (approx. 60 employees) and NOVAK CZECH (approx. 120 employees). The seller (who also owned the company LIMET) wanted to continue to procure and sell the products. The buyers wanted to develop the company from an extended workbench to an independent company. They expected that the acquired know-how and structures would lead to quick and cost-efficient independence for NOVAK CZECH from NOVAK AUSTRIA (its affiliate) and thus to greater value creation.

NOVAK CZECH has existed since 1992 with its head office in Brünn, the Czech Republic, and has belonged since its founding to the Austrian group Josef Novak Beteiligungs-AG. The direct 100% owner of NOVAK is the Novak Holding Group GmbH, with NOVAK HOLDING functioning as a holding company for multiple companies of the Josef Novak group. The group is 100% owned by the Novak family.[5]

JERMAN, the company being sold, was founded in 1996 with its head office in Dolany, near Prague, Czech Republic. In addition to JERMAN, the

---

5 Cf. Annual Report of Josef Novak Beteiligungs-AG dated 31.12.2003, p. 4, NOVAK Controlling.

owner, an Austrian citizen, headed a distribution company in Wels, Austria, called Linz Metall GmbH (LIMET), which deals in the distribution of sheet metal forming products[6].

2.2 The planned competitive advantage to be obtained through the upward revaluation of the extended workbench

Lower production costs in Eastern Europe caused a separation of corporate management and operative production, the latter of which moved toward the east. Both the seller and the buyers benefitted from the political turnaround of the early 1990s and from labor cost advantages by producing in the Czech Republic.[7] NOVAK CZECH served as an extended workbench for its affiliate NOVAK AUSTRIA, which had its head offices in Vienna. Until 2003, 100% of NOVAK CZECH's business activity consisted of functioning as a supplier for NOVAK AUSTRIA. In the 1990s, the extended workbench gave NOVAK AUSTRIA the advantage of low Czech labor costs, which in 1992, the year in which NOVAK was founded, were around 25% to 30% lower than in Austria.[8]

Until 2003 NOVAK CZECH manufactured simple[9] die cutting and welding products. Technicians from NOVAK AUSTRIA resolved problems at NOVAK CZECH. Raw materials were also centrally procured by NOVAK AUSTRIA. The business areas remaining with NOVAK CZECH were production, dealing with companies providing linings and coatings (materials management) and local accounting. When Bulgaria, Rumania and Ukraine entered Western markets at the end of the 1990s, NOVAK CZECH lost the positive effect of being an extended workbench, since their new competitors offered even lower labor costs than the Czech Republic did. Based on this, the owners (the Novak family) decided to acquire JERMAN, which in comparison to NOVAK CZECH had the advantage of a more complex product portfolio with higher added value and more know-how.[10]

---

6 The company LIMET was simultaneously the legal owner of JERMAN.
7 Cf. Interview with Andreas Linz (owner of JERMAN and LIMET) on 08.03.2010.
8 Cf. Interview with Wolfgang Frey (Technical Director of NOVAK, Project Manager of Integration), recorded on 04.03.2010.
9 In this context, "simple products" refers to those whose manufacture involves few steps, requires simple know-how from the workers and features rather paternalistic-hierarchical structures and leadership requirements.
10 In this context, "added value" is understood to mean production costs expressed as a proportion of the price of the product. High personnel costs have a negative ef-

2.3 The complexity of the products, production and customer relations

JERMAN's products, production processes and interaction with customers were all more complex. The preparation of an offer to purchase was based on preliminary calculations with planned costs, number of working hours and material use. A dedicated department with technicians prepared this offer.[11] This complexity of products and customer relations required additional knowledge and a high level of cooperation. The necessary personnel management and corporate management overtaxed JERMAN's paternalistic management concepts, which, according to the owner, compelled the sale:

> "I managed the entire course of events at JERMAN. I acquired all contracts and set the resulting priorities. This was the main reason I had to sell the company, as I did not have the time to handle both customer acquisition and the operative management tasks in production. The production workers exhibited a lack of decision-making capacity with reference to further inquiries, complaints and production supply shortfalls, which led to massive problems in the processes and, as a result, in the deliverables."[12]

2.4 Sale and contract design as formation of a cooperation (7/2002–2/2003)

The owner of JERMAN (Andreas Linz) had been looking for a buyer for the company since the middle of 2002. Contact with the Novak family was made through a consulting firm. After multiple visits and a comprehensive economic examination of the company by the management of the Novak group, NOVAK CZECH purchased JERMAN. A pivotal requirement by the seller (Andreas Linz, owner of JERMAN and LIMET) for the sale to NOVAK CZECH was the guaranteed continuation of the hitherto existing production by the buyer, since the buyer's Austrian company LIMET was economi-

---

fect on prices because the production costs are higher; thus the company's results deteriorate.

11 Cf. Minutes of the project meeting attended by Peter Novak (owner) and Christian Steindl (Managing Director of NOVAK) and Wolfgang Frey (technician at NOVAK AUSTRIA) on 12.01.2003, NOVAK Controlling.
12 Interview with Andreas Linz (owner of JERMAN and LIMET), recorded on 08.03.2010.

cally dependent on the sale of these products.[13] The general conditions[14] for the sale were:

- NOVAK CZECH will sell JERMAN, including all its assets, with effective date 31.12.2002.
- JERMAN in its previous form as a company will be liquidated by the buyer.[15]
- NOVAK CZECH will enlarge its location in Brünn and relocate the production line with all machines, technical facilities, factory equipment and office furniture and equipment from Dolany to Brünn.
- NOVAK CZECH obligates itself to supply the company LIMET for a period of at least five years.
- During the five-year period of commitment, LIMET may only buy the products from other suppliers if those suppliers' prices are lower than NOVAK CZECH's prices. Before changing suppliers, LIMET must give NOVAK CZECH the opportunity to amend its prices.

The contract of sale was signed on 17 February 2003 upon the above-mentioned conditions. On the same day the preparations for the integration and the relocation of JERMAN to NOVAK in Brünn were begun.[16]

2.5 Evaluation and planning of the requirements for the consolidation of the companies (3–5/2003)

The planning and execution of the project was carried out by a small NOVAK CZECH project team led by Wolfgang Frey, a technical project manager who already worked for both NOVAK AUSTRIA and NOVAK CZECH. After the project team had visited JERMAN several times, the following points were identified and prioritized as critical areas for the integration of JERMAN into NOVAK CZECH:[17]

1. Transferring the existing JERMAN technicians' know-how relating to process design and submission of quotations for customers.
2. Cooperation between the workers from NOVAK CZECH and those from JERMAN in complex productions.

---

13 Cf. Interview with Andreas Linz (owner of JERMAN and LIMET), recorded on 08.03.2010.
14 Cf. Excerpt from the contract of sale dated 17.03.2003, NOVAK Controlling.
15 To clarify, this means that the company JERMAN no longer existed from that point in time.
16 Cf. Sales contract dated 17.03.2003, NOVAK Controlling.
17 Cf. Project plan dated 03.04.2003, NOVAK Controlling.

3. Hiring qualified production workers for the relocated computer-operated machines for sheet metal forming in Brünn.
4. Training qualified workers in the technology and sales areas.
5. Acquiring an integrated EDP system to support the operative processes in all essential internal functional areas and represent the increased complexity (finance, accounting, materials management, production, sales).

3 The creation of solutions (10/2003–12/2006)

3.1 Solution 1: Transfer of knowledge from JERMAN to NOVAK CZECH (10/2003–3/2005)

The relocation of production from Dolany to Brünn took place from October to December 2003. In spring and summer 2003 NOVAK CZECH built an additional production hall. From the end of December 2003 production took place and JERMAN's existing customers were supplied from Brünn.[18]

At the end of 2003, NOVAK CZECH made a takeover bid to JERMAN's experts; three technicians accepted the bid for the period from December 2003 through July 2005. The technicians' assignment was to pass on to the workers in Brünn their product-related know-how and experience in calculations for customers. The cooperation between the three technicians from JERMAN and the existing workers in Brünn proved difficult in practice. In the first place, there were no NOVAK CZECH workers in Brünn who were sufficiently qualified as technicians to be able to take over the know-how of JERMAN's experts. Further, it was difficult for JERMAN's technicians to communicate customer requirements regarding production to NOVAK CZECH's production workers.[19]

The result was a decrease in total order quantity and an associated reduction in turnover. The performance data for 2004 were surprisingly low;[20] surprising, because much higher operating results had been expected based on the planning.[21] Management saw two causes for the unsatisfactory operating results:[22]

---

18 Cf. Comparison of budget figures with actual figures, project plan dated 08.12.2003, NOVAK Controlling.
19 Cf. Interim Report by Project Leader Wolfgang Frey to the Management Board dated 03.02.2004, NOVAK Controlling.
20 Cf. Annual Report NOVAK 2004, NOVAK Controlling.
21 Cf. Budget planning NOVAK 2004, NOVAK Controlling.
22 Cf. Minutes of the Meeting of the Management Boards of NOVAK and NOVAK Holding on 19.03.2005, NOVAK Controlling.

- A lack of expertise in NOVAK CZECH's technical and sales areas.
- A lack of EDP instruments capable of representing product calculations, so that results for individual products and orders could be worked out.

3.2 Solution 2: Shift in priorities–sales expertise from the market and EDP integration (3/2005–10/2005)

In March 2005 the management of NOVAK CZECH realized that points 4 and 5 of the project plan had received too little attention and reordered their priorities so that the following two measures were emphasized:[23]

3.2.1 Speed up the hiring of qualified workers in the technical and sales areas[24]

The search for sales personnel began in March 2005. In May 2005 two qualified employees for in-house sales were hired,[25] and in July one employee in external sales.[26] With these sales reps NOVAK CZECH's direct sales force was established, with the intention of further strengthening the company's independence. This buildup, however, did not result in the desired quality, which led to terminations and new hirings.[27] In October 2005 NOVAK CZECH succeeded in hiring a technical sales rep from Austria who had been very successfully selling their products in Austria and Germany since earlier that year.[28] Through this employee's efforts NOVAK's turnover rose by 57% in the years from 2005 to 2009.[29]

The hiring of new workers in the technical area happened more quickly because there were more qualified candidates in the Czech employment market. Two technicians had already been hired at the end of 2004. Due to the increased focus on building up the technical area, in March 2005 additional employees were hired for the work preparation and programming of the CNC machines (computerized numerical control). Some of them were

---

23 Cf. Minutes of the meeting of the Management Boards of NOVAK and NOVAK Holding on 19.03.2005 – point 5, NOVAK Controlling.
24 See point 4 of the list of priorities under 2.5.
25 Cf. Sales payroll 2004, NOVAK Controlling.
26 Cf. Sales payroll 2004, NOVAK Controlling.
27 Cf. Personnel changes in sales from May 2004, NOVAK Controlling.
28 Cf. Sales payroll 2004, NOVAK Controlling.
29 Cf. NOVAK turnover statistics of 31.12.2009, NOVAK Controlling.

terminated due to lack of qualifications for the complex products. In addition, a design engineer was hired. The following table shows the buildup of expertise in the technical area and in comparison to the number of employees in the entire company from 2004 to 2006.[30]

	2004	2005	2006
NOVAK employees in the technical area (= work preparation, CNC programming and construction)	6	8	8
JERMAN employees in the technical area (commuting between Prague and Brünn)	3	3 (through mid-2005)	0
NOVAK employees overall	193	191	149

Table 1: NOVAK employees in the technical area and overall in the years 2004 and 2006. Source: NOVAK Personnel Department.

3.2.2 The acquisition of an integrated EDP system to support operative processes (6/2004– 6/2005)

Parallel to the buildup of technical expertise, Project NOVAX was begun and the integrated EDP system for finance, accounting, materials management, production and sales was installed. In the process, NOVAK CZECH from the NOVAK HOLDING and the EDP department of the parent company of the group, the Josef Novak Beteiligungs-AG, were supported. After several days of process analyses, the choice fell on Microsoft's system Axapta 3.0 due to its strong cost-benefit analysis.[31] The contracts with the implementation partner were signed in June 2004, and the start date for live operation was planned for January 2005.

During the launch of this system difficulties arose; organizational structuring and operational structuring were not sufficiently consolidated: on the one hand, missing decisions by local workers, on the other hand, regular posting errors through faulty data flows. Nonetheless, the implementation began in January 2005.

---

30 Cf. Technology payroll 2004, NOVAK Controlling.
31 Cf. Presentation on comparison of solutions ERP system of the EDP department of the group dated 22.06.2004, NOVAK Controlling.

"The decision ... was basically right. What was not right was the timing of the implementation, because ... the organizational weakness during the implementation had nearly scuppered the project, which created serious difficulties for the company. On the one hand, a large number of employees were too heavily involved with the system itself and with the new modes of operation; on the other hand, they had lost sight of the fact that profit margins were declining, or rather, the new product mix made different demands on pricing policy than previous products had. For a project such as the first-time introduction of an ERP system, organizational responsibilities and process data flows absolutely must be known in advance to all participants and must be clearly defined. Nevertheless, in the end the project was positively implemented and, according to a previous colleague, has so far proved itself."[32] (Managing Director of NOVAK until 2005)

At six months, the time between the start of the project and its implementation was short; motivation and commitment of the key users were low. There was significant involvement in the top-down introduction by the Managing Director, Andreas Segen, and the Project Leader of Project NOVAK from the parent company NOVAK HOLDING, Hannes Holzer.[33] In July 2005 the first end-of-month accounts (finance) from the EDP system (ERP system) were generated; operating results to 30.06.2005[34] disclosed a loss of CZK 10 m (approximately EUR 400,000 at an exchange rate of EUR 1 = CZK 25). At the beginning of 2006 the processes of sales, production, materials management and finance were satisfactorily represented and results and measures derived.[35]

3.3 Solution 3: Management shifts (9/2005–2/2006)

Due to the unsatisfactory operating results in 2004 and 2005, the owners decided the first two solutions had failed and laid the blame for failure on the management board of NOVAK CZECH. In the course of the supervisory board meeting in September 2005 the owners terminated the contract of the Managing Director, Andreas Segen.[36] This termination came as a sur-

---

32 Interview with Andreas Segen (Managing Director of NOVAK until 2005), recorded on 08.03.2010.
33 Cf. Interim Report by the Project Director dated 19.09.2004, NOVAK Controlling.
34 Cf. NOVAK's Interim Balance Sheet of 30.06.2005, NOVAK Controlling.
35 Cf. E-mail from the Project Leader Hannes Holzer to the Managing Director Christian Steindl dated 08.01.2006, NOVAK Controlling.
36 Cf. Minutes of the supervisory board meeting on 16.08.2005, NOVAK Controlling.

prise to him, since he was still convinced that he and his team could overcome the difficulties.[37] In an interview he mentioned that the organization had had trouble adjusting to the changed processes, and the owners had as a result lost confidence in his abilities. He saw the cooperation problems with his Co-Managing Director as decisive in this; there had been differences of opinion about the approaches to problem solving. The solution to communication-problems in management was to blame other people; i.e. passing the buck–shoving responsibility off on others.

In his position as Managing Director of Finance, Christian Steindl intervened and fired the previous controller of NOVAK AUSTRIA and NOVAK CZECH. As successor he chose the project leader for the implementation of the ERP system, Hannes Holzer, who had previously worked for NOVAK HOLDING, to be responsible for the areas controlling, EDP, materials management and quality management for NOVAK CZECH and its sister company NOVAK AUSTRIA.[38]

The Managing Director Christian Steindl (simultaneously Managing Director of NOVAK CZECH) promoted the project leader of the merger to general manager and division manager for technology and sales, and transferred the employee Gerhard Walek from NOVAK AUSTRIA to NOVAK CZECH with responsibility for production. As a result, in Brünn, the Czech Republic, the responsible managers were Wolfgang Frey for technology and sales, Gerhard Walek for production, and Hannes Holzer for controlling, IT, finance, personnel, materials management and quality management. These three were each responsible for the same areas in the sister company NOVAK AUSTRIA.[39] Steindl worked to a large extent from Vienna.

These shifts led to the following organigram for NOVAK CZECH (p. 35).

A note at this point: the sole Managing Director of NOVAK HOLDING[40] was simultaneously Managing Director of NOVAK and NOVAK AUSTRIA and was, de facto, his own supervisor. Contact at the top was tightly hierarchically structured. The threefold Managing Director had sole contact to the owners.

---

37 Cf. Interview with Andreas Segen, Managing Director of NOVAK through 2005, dated 08.03.2010.
38 Cf. Personnel Bulletin 29 of NOVAK HOLDING dated 31.08.2005, NOVAK Controlling.
39 Cf. Personnel Bulletin 31 of NOVAK HOLDING dated 26.08.2005, NOVAK Controlling.
40 Cf. Excerpt from commercial register NOVAK HOLDING dated 31.10.2003, NOVAK Controlling.

**Organigram
NOVAK CZECH**

```
                    Managing Director
                    Christian Steindl
                 General Manager: Wolfgang Frey
                    │              │
         Controlling / IT    Quality Management
         Hannes Holzer       Hannes Holzer
    ┌──────────┬──────────┬──────────┬──────────┐
   Sales    Technology  Production  Materials   Finance/Personnel
  Wolfgang  Wolfgang    Gerhard     Management  Hannes Holzer
   Frey     Frey        Walek       Hannes Holzer
```

Figure 2: Organigram of NOVAK CZECH 2005, Source: NOVAK CZECH Controlling

After a few weeks, finger-pointing began within management[41]. When communicating with the owners, Christian Steindl laid the blame for problems at the feet of the new management working under him. This continued the pattern that he had practiced during his work with his previous Co-Managing Director Andreas Segen; it was a pattern which hindered the search to identify and solve problems. Because working together was so difficult, nothing could be improved.

Because of these difficulties, Wolfgang Frey resigned in October 2005,[42] leaving the sister company NOVAK AUSTRIA without a Director of Sales and Technology. The Managing Director Christian Steindl decided to look for a Director of Sales. In January 2006 Sigmund Scharner took over this position in NOVAK. At that time he was 54 years old and had many years of experience in the fields of metalworking and sheet metal forming.[43] The area of technology was added to the portfolio of the Director of Production, Gerhard Walek[44].

The balance sheet for 2005, issued in February 2006, showed negative surprises in operating results: a loss of CZK 34 m (approximately EUR 1.3 m). Annual turnover of CZK 304 m (approximately EUR 12.1 m) showed a

---

41 In this context, "management" refers to those named in the organigram.
42 Cf. Interview with Wolfgang Frey, Project Leader for Integration and Director of Technology at NOVAK.
43 Cf. Personnel Bulletin 36 of NOVAK HOLDING dated 06.01.2006, NOVAK Controlling.
44 Cf. Minutes of the management meeting on 03.11.2005, point 1, NOVAK Controlling.

return (operating results in relation to annual turnover) of minus 11.3%.[45] The result of personnel shifts within management, the problems of cooperation among the managers, and the loss of a manager who had worked for the company for many years had combined to lead to deterioration in results within only a few months. In an interview, Wolfgang Frey,[46] (the former Director of Sales and Technology) attributed the problems at that time to insufficient problem-solving skills on the part of management:

> "The Austrian management did not succeed in establishing on-site a functioning organization with stable structures and processes which was in a position to press ahead with solving the problems which occurred. The Austrian management's most important task should have been to find and develop good local managers."[47]

The idea that simply replacing individual people would bring the desired success in the form of improved operating results is a mechanical approach. It showed that at that time the owners had a shortsighted focus on current results and figures. The owners had taken an active role in terminating Andreas Segen; exclusively Christian Steindl had communicated sufficient reason for the decision to them. This demonstrates that the owners and management of the company oriented themselves along the hierarchical structure. The departure of Wolfgang Frey, Director of Technology and Sales, had not been planned by the Managing Director Steindl but could not have been avoided and points to one possible effect of this finger-pointing hierarchical management pattern: a competent manager left the company.

3.4 Solution 4: The putsch against the Austrian hierarchical system (1/2006–6/2006)

At the beginning of 2006 Sigmund Scharner took over as Director of Sales for NOVAK. He too was responsible for NOVAK CZECH and NOVAK AUSTRIA.[48] At the start, in close cooperation with Gerhard Walek and Hannes Holzer, he obtained an overview, analyzed the products and initiated first measures. This analysis was possible because at the beginning of 2006 mean-

---

45 Cf. Balance Sheet NOVAK dated 31.12.2005, NOVAK Controlling.
46 The interview took place on 04.03.2010, more than four years later.
47 Interview with Wolfgang Frey, Project Leader for Integration and Director of Technology for NOVAK, recorded on 04.03.2010.
48 Like all other members of management.

ingful results from the new EDP system could be evaluated for the first time. The measures were:[49]

- Analysis of products and customers
- Pre and post calculations for products
- Price negotiations with suppliers
- Price negotiations with customers
- Analysis of processes within the organization

He saw filling management positions (area directors) with Austrian managers as one of the biggest hurdles, the result of which being that local experts and managers were not involved in decisions and thus did not identify with them. His suggestion for changing the organization was rejected by the Managing Director Steindl because the latter did not want to accept any Czech managers, giving as his reason the language barrier.[50]

As time went on the problems within the management team between the top level (Managing Director Steindl) and the second level (Directors: Scharner, Sales; Walek, Technology; Holzer, Controlling, EDP, Finance, Personnel, Materials Management, Quality Management) escalated. The situation was characterized by accusations.[51] Due to the continuing difficulties in cooperation, the Managing Director Steindl fired Gerhard Walek, the Director of Technology. As a result Sigmund Scharner (Sales) also took over responsibility for the areas of technology and production. Cooperation within management deteriorated again dramatically.

Sigmund Scharner (Sales, Production) requested a face-to-face meeting with the owners in June 2006. After hearing his description of the problems, the owners decided to remove Christian Steindl immediately as Managing Director of the companies NOVAK and NOVAK AUSTRIA. Sigmund Scharner and Hannes Holzer became the Managing Directors of the two sister companies NOVAK CZECH and NOVAK AUSTRIA. This step was essential for NOVAK CZECH: the owners' contact with the responsible people at NOVAK had changed. For the first time, the owners accepted direct contact with the area managers, thus opening up a second perspective.

---

[49] Cf. Minutes of the management meeting of NOVAK on 28.01.2006; point 2, NOVAK Controlling.
[50] Cf. Minutes of the management meeting of NOVAK on 27.02.2006; point 2, NOVAK Controlling.
[51] Cf. Note for the files by Sigmund Scharner (Director of Sales) regarding a meeting between Christian Steindl (Managing Director) and Sigmund Scharner (Director of Sales) on 17.04.2006, Sigmund Scharner.

3.5 Solution 5: Slow buildup of independence and complexity (from 6/2006)

3.5.1 Buildup of a local Czech area management

The new Managing Directors Scharner and Holzer abandoned the previous path of using Austrian managers and filled the positions of area managers with locals. In the run-up to this, the two Managing Directors conducted discussions for several weeks with people in the know in companies in order to spot potential.[52] Sigmund Scharner interpreted this step as a central factor for success:

> "Filling the area manager positions with locals rather than with Austrians was probably the best decision that the new management made, and it was made for two reasons. On the one hand, the cost factor was important, since Austrian managers in general earned multiple times as much [as Czech managers]; second, we wanted to destroy the existing divide between Austrians and Czechs, which at that time was very pronounced."[53]

He had in mind the concept of the long-term perspective of a slow buildup and implemented this together with Holzer, the other Managing Director:

> "It was clear to us that these changes were not a revolutionary step, but rather that many small measures would have to follow in order for the pieces of the puzzle to fit together and lead to success. Holzer and I were a good team; we both wanted to initiate new perspectives and possibilities for management."[54]

3.5.2 Divided responsibility and language training ensure development of the complete perspective and an information base for all

The two new Managing Directors immediately began to hold weekly meetings with the area managers for technology, sales, quality, production and

---

52 Interview with Sigmund Scharner, Managing Director of NOVAK from 2006, recorded on 06.03.2010.
53 Interview with Sigmund Scharner, Managing Director of NOVAK from 2006, recorded on 06.03.2010.
54 Interview with Sigmund Scharner, Managing Director of NOVAK from 2006, recorded on 06.03.2010.

finance. The meetings were held in German and translated when necessary. The subjects were assigned to the people in the company who represented and worked with them. Thus the local managers were directly involved and the local workers in Brünn indirectly involved in the decisions and developments, and information was made available to everyone in Czech.[55]

Free language courses in German and English were a further step in reducing communication difficulties. Simultaneously the two Austrian Managing Directors began to learn Czech. The following table shows the increase in the number of employees who took part during their free time:

German courses

	2005	2006	2007
Total number of employees as of 31 December	191	149	161
Number of employees participating in courses	4	28	51
Percentage of the entire staff participating in courses	2.1%	18.8%	31.7%

Table 2: NOVAK employees participating in German courses 2005 to 2007, Source: NOVAK Personnel Department

English courses

	2005	2006	2007
Total number of employees as of 31 December	191	14,783	16,818
Number of employees participating in courses	0	6	19
Percentage of the entire staff participating in courses	0%	4.0%	11.8%

Table 3: NOVAK employees participating in English courses 2005 to 2007, Source: NOVAK Personnel Department

---

55 Cf. Minutes of the management meeting on 17.08.2006.

3.5.3 Quality awareness: management and customer support

To increase product and process quality, Jaroslav Janas was hired as Quality Manager in July 2006 with two central areas of responsibility: first, the implementation and standardization of the management system ISO 9001, above all sustainably to anchor the management and core processes,[56] and second, to increase the production workers'[57] and customer support agents' quality awareness. A local worker from the Quality Department was called in on larger customer complaints, which enabled the production workers to form a picture for themselves of customer needs and requirements.[58] The result was a reduction in the cost of complaints from more than EUR 520,000 in 2005 to EUR 92,000 in 2007.

	2005	2006	2007
Turnover in thousands of EUR	12,158	14,783	16,818
Cost of complaints in thousands of EUR	525	230	94
Cost of complaints as a percentage of turnover	4.31%	1.55%	0.56%

Table 4: Development of cost of complaints NOVAK 2005 to 2007, Source: NOVAK Controlling

3.5.4 Cooperative future-oriented management with simultaneous decisive measures (from 8/2006)

The management considered that in the current situation (8/2006) a financial restructuring program[59] was essential for the company's survival. The decisive core measures were:

- Reducing the number of employees from 191 to 149 in 2006.[60]

---

56 Cf. Job description Quality Manager dated 01.07.2007, Personnel Department NOVAK.
57 Cf. Job description Quality Manager dated 01.07.2007, Personnel Department NOVAK.
58 Cf. Minutes of the management meeting on 22.07.2007, Point 4, NOVAK Controlling.
59 Cf. Interview with Sigmund Scharner, Managing Director of NOVAK from 2006.
60 In 2007, due to increased turnover, workers were hired again in manufacturing.

- Introducing a continuous, consumption-driven production process; repetition parts.
- Streamlining the supply structure and optimizing the purchase price of materials.
- Optimizing the product pallet and reducing the customer portfolio from 260 customers to around 100 customers through elimination of economically unviable customers.
- Introducing complex welding constructions and montage products into the production program[61].

The management team was constituted and went through the cutbacks and reorganization together:

> Managing Director Scharner: "As unpleasant as these measures in 2006 were, above all the cutbacks in employees, we were able to master and overcome these unpleasant and difficult steps through cooperation with the local management team and the workers."[62]

Director of Production Peter Prybil, in whose area the most changes took place:

> "In my function as Director of Production I was responsible for the highest number of workers. Many of them were and are simple workers without a high level of education. 2006 was associated with many unpleasant steps for NOVAK, which above all had direct influence on the workers in my area. For the first time in my many years with NOVAK I was directly involved in the decisions and felt completely informed. For this reason I was significantly better prepared for the implementation of the layoff of workers, and during the discussions I had facts and figures at my fingertips with which I could justify the decisions. The decision itself was the same; however, as its executor the determining factors were, for me, on a qualitatively higher level. At this point a jolt ran through the entire team of managers and workers in Brünn. The previous division between Austrians and Czechs was vastly reduced; the area of conflict became a common path."[63]

---

61 Due to higher labor input in combination with the lower wage level, NOVAK was able to realize a higher profit margin for these products. In addition, NOVAK succeeded in becoming a certified welding company.
62 Interview with Sigmund Scharner, Managing Director of NOVAK from 2006.
63 Interview with Peter Prybil, Director of Production at NOVAK, recorded on 12.03.2010.

3.5.5 Medium-term effects of the establishment of independence (2007–2010)

The 2006 operating results of NOVAK CZECH were positive for the first time, which pleased the owners and was therefore good for the entire team. From 2006 to 2009 increases were recorded.[64] In response to a question about the current status, the Managing Director Sigmund Scharner said in March 2010:

> "The company has developed greatly in recent years. Turnover and operating results have increased rapidly; in this process, the inclusion of local management has proved to be very important and necessary. The internal processes are functioning to a large extent satisfactorily and are organized. Nevertheless, despite all efforts, the company and its management have not succeeded in getting the employees, most especially the local managers, to demonstrate farsightedness and future-oriented thinking. New ideas, new product developments and acquisition of new international customers are still predominantly initiated through the executive management. This is problematic in that it severely ties up their resources. The potential capacities, which are lost because of limited contact with new markets by the managers and workers represent a high risk for the further growth of the company. That is the next leverage which must be applied."[65]

The fifth attempt at a solution, developing the organization and workers towards independence by a package of multiple measures, was the decisive and successful approach to setting the organization on a course which would bring with it positive operating results. Through the change in perspective to long-term thinking in management, the owners' short-term monetary goals were also met. In other words, the numbers did not develop satisfactorily until after the transformation in the integration phase.

4 Scenarios for the future

The story told here shows us the company at a fork in the road after the turbulence of recent years; new perspectives and forms of cooperation at the first and second levels of management have developed, but not sufficiently to be consolidated as carriers of culture. In which directions could

---

64 Cf. Annual Reports NOVAK from 2006 to 2009, NOVAK Controlling.
65 Interview with Sigmund Scharner, Managing Director of NOVAK from 2006, recorded on 06.03.2010.

the company NOVAK CZECH hypothetically develop, based on this situation? Below are two possibilities presented with the help of two scenarios, a "lose" scenario and a "win" scenario.

4.1 Integrative, meaningful forms of cooperation are lost again

Sigmund Scharner's appointment as Managing Director of NOVAK must be considered as a key success factor. Together with Hannes Holzer and the local managers he set up a framework in which economic[66] success became possible. Above all this was due to the cooperative management style and the associated consideration of various perspectives within the cooperation. Sigmund Scharner embodies the paternal role of the supporter and all-knowing technician, which on the one hand reflects the hierarchical logic but simultaneously opens up new possibilities. He can bridge between the hierarchical and cooperative styles of management and thus provide the necessary balance between the different cultures.

He is 59 years old, so in a few years he will transition into retirement. In recent years the managers and workers at NOVAK have achieved rapid development; nonetheless, Sigmund Scharner now as then takes over the integrative part of management. The fifth solution presented shows that the company was missing important elements of the social and cultural subsystems of a holistic organization during the first four attempts. If it does not succeed in adequately filling this function of integrated management or transferring it to the complete system, then, despite all the groundwork, there is the threat of a relapse into the old exclusive, hierarchical pattern. The second Managing Director, Hannes Holzer, 40 years of age, could theoretically further the new culture, but in the hierarchically structured business practice, which still exists in the company, the technological management still plays a central role.

If there were interference by the holding company and owners, the basic values, which have been built up could come apart at the seams. Two possible ways to lose what has been acquired would be a change of management or the sale of the company NOVAK CZECH by the owners. No one could predict at this point which values and culture a buyer would bring into the company and how this would affect the company NOVAK.

---

66 And human successes. To deal with these is beyond the scope of this case.

4.2 Cooperation, responsibility and collective learning continue to develop

The continuation of the previous groundwork can shape the local management and the workers with its positive flow through its development demands on individuals. They continue to grasp the development demands as individuals and system. What they have experienced together is transformed into mutual learning and is anchored as such in the system. With reference to the development phases of Glasl & Lievegoed, the company NOVAK CZECH can be assigned to the integration phase.[67] A majority of the managers and workers have experienced the previous short-term perspective orientation and the change to a cooperative, long-term perspective with its associated economic successes.

Through the stabilization of the "soft facts"[68] the diversity and the cultural differences among the people were respected. The two Managing Directors changed the understanding in the company of how to behave, communicate and learn with others. In the positive scenario, the basic principles of cooperative management are internalized. The management and cooperation culture is maintained and becomes a point of orientation for new workers and parts of the company. Together the future can be actively formed instead of passively experienced, and independence and profits increased.

5 Summary of interpretation

Due to the sale of JERMAN and the demands associated with the transformation from an extended workbench to an independent company, extensive changes in the management and organization of NOVAK CZECH became necessary. The solutions resulted from trial and error, the interpretation of errors and the learning that came from them. This path was associated with problems for management and with unsatisfactory results.

Solutions 1 through 4[69] identified a mechanical understanding of management and change, which generated short-term solutions. The Managing Directors Andreas Segen and Christian Steindl tried to compensate for lack of specialist knowledge by installing experts in the areas of technology and

---

67 See further Glasl F./Lievegoed B. 2004.
68 Which in this case we experienced as the actual "hard facts".
69 See 3.1 to 3.4 in this paper.

sales and by a technical solution–the introduction of an integrated EDP system. Due to its one-dimensional hierarchical system, the company could not see clearly enough to set up complex conditions of the consolidation. The owners were not actively involved in the definition of priorities and their implementation, but rather this was accomplished by the hierarchically higher-ranking control of the Managing Director of NOVAK CZECH of the NOVAK HOLDING. Change of perspective and the negotiation of interests got a raw deal.

In Solution 5 a shift occurred in that the relationship of the owners to the management of NOVAK CZECH and to NOVAK HOLDING changed. The area managers presented their own perspective to the owners. The owners allowed the Managing Directors Scharner and Holzer a new attempt. The new pair of managing directors seized the opportunity and made dramatic changes. The change in management style, the cooperative pair of leaders, the development of an area manager team, and the move from centralized management from Austria to cooperative management with local managers created the basis for complex forms of cooperation in management, in cooperation among the experts and with customers. NOVAK CZECH was able to interpret and experience itself as an independent company for the first time. The area managers became part of the management team and were no longer simply the extended arm of the owners. NOVAK AUSTRIA[70] was no longer present in the management of its sister company NOVAK CZECH. NOVAK CZECH was able to build up an independent identity. This development was essential for the company in order to keep its performance in the sense of an active organization as a system from becoming dependent on individual people in this hierarchical dimension.

Index of tables

Table 1: NOVAK employees in the technical area and overall in the years 2004 and 2006. Source: NOVAK Personnel Department.

Table 2: NOVAK employees participating in German courses 2005 to 2007, Source: NOVAK Personnel Department

Table 3: NOVAK employees participating in English courses 2005 to 2007, Source: NOVAK Personnel Department

Table 4: Development of cost of complaints NOVAK 2005 to 2007, Source: NOVAK Controlling

---

70 With the exception of one Managing Director.

Index of figures

Figure 1: Overview of the companies involved

Figure 2: Organigram of NOVAK CZECH 2005, Source: NOVAK CZECH Controlling

Index of abbreviations

CZ	The Czech Republic
CZK	Czech Crowns (the currency of the Czech Republic); Exchange rate used: EUR 1 = CZK 25
NOVAK CZECH	Novak Metal s.r.o.
NOVAK AUSTRIA	Novak Metall GmbH
NOVAK HOLDING	Novak Group Holding GmbH
JERMAN	Jerman s.r.o.
LIMET	Linz Metall GmbH

References and empirical sources

Annual Report NOVAK 2004, NOVAK Controlling.

Annual Report of Josef Novak Beteiligungs-AG dated 31.12.2003, NOVAK Controlling.

Annual Reports NOVAK from 2006 to 2009, NOVAK Controlling.

Balance Sheet NOVAK 31.12.2005, NOVAK Controlling.

Budget planning NOVAK 2004, NOVAK Controlling.

Comparison of budget figures with actual figures, project plan dated 08.12.2003, NOVAK Controlling.

Contract of Sale dated 17.03.2003, NOVAK Controlling.

E-mail from the Project Leader Hannes Holzer to the Managing Director Christian Steindl dated 08.01.2006, NOVAK Controlling.

Glasl F./Lievegoed B., 2004, Dynamische Unternehmensentwicklung. Grundlagen für nachhaltiges Change Management, 3rd revised and expanded edition, Haupt Verlag, Bern/Stuttgart/Vienna, Verlag Freies Geistesleben, Stuttgart.

Interim Report by Project Leader Wolfgang Frey to the Management Board dated 03.02.2004, NOVAK Controlling.

Interim Report by the Project Director dated 19.09.2004, NOVAK Controlling.

Interview with Wolfgang Frey (Director of Technology NOVAK, Project Leader for Integration), 04.03.2010.

Interview with Sigmund Scharner (Managing Director NOVAK from 2006), 06.03.2010.

Interview with Andreas Linz (owner of JERMAN and LIMET), 08.03.2010.

Interview with Andreas Segen (Managing Director NOVAK through 2005), 08.03.2010.

Interview with Peter Prybil (Director of Production NOVAK), 12.03.2010.

Job description Quality Manager dated 01.07.2007, Personnel Department NOVAK.

Minutes of the project meeting attended by Peter Novak (owner), Christian Steindl (Managing Director of NOVAK) and Wolfgang Frey (Technician at NOVAK AUSTRIA) on 12.01.2003; NOVAK Controlling.

Minutes of the meeting of the Management Boards of NOVAK and NOVAK Holding on 19.03.2005; NOVAK Controlling.

Minutes of the meeting of the supervisory board on 16.08.2005, NOVAK Controlling.

Minutes of the management meeting on 03.11.2005; NOVAK Controlling.

Minutes of the management meeting of NOVAK on 28.01.2006; NOVAK Controlling.

Minutes of the management meeting on 06.02.2006; NOVAK Controlling.

Minutes of the management meeting of NOVAK on 27.02.2006; NOVAK Controlling.

Minutes of the management meeting on 17.08.2006.

NOVAK turnover statistics of 31.12.2009, NOVAK Controlling.

NOVAK's Interim Balance Sheet of 30.06.2005, NOVAK Controlling.

Personnel Bulletin 29 of NOVAK HOLDING, 31.08.2005, NOVAK Controlling.

Personnel Bulletin 31 of NOVAK HOLDING, 26.09.2005, NOVAK Controlling.

Personnel Bulletin 36 of NOVAK HOLDING, 06.01.2006, NOVAK Controlling.

Presentation on comparison of solutions ERP system of the EDP department of the group dated 22.06.2004, NOVAK Controlling.

Project plan, 03.04.2003, NOVAK Controlling.

Sales payroll 2004, NOVAK Controlling.

Technology payroll 2004, NOVAK Controlling.

Natasa Ilic, MBA

Institutionalisation and strategic focus of Public Relations (PR) at the Volksbank Serbia

The path from informal to institutionalised PR work based on the example of the establishment of the Volksbank Serbia

Introduction

In the following case study the development and focus of public relations (PR)[1] at the Volksbank Serbia from its founding in 2003 through 2008 will be examined and highlighted. The case study illustrates the background to and specific connections between the institutionalisation and organisational establishment of this field of activity in the bank and the career of the Public Relations Manager. The context of the case therefore lies in an organisational (implementation of PR) and personal (career of the PR Manager) framework within the political and economic environment (the nation of Serbia) and the market (banking).

The political and economic conditions and circumstances in Serbia at the time the bank was founded played a significant role in the development of public relations in the bank. At that time Serbia was in a period of rapid transition from a centrally controlled command economy to a free market economy[2] (designated as "Environment" in Illustration 1).

The newly founded Volksbank Serbia had a Marketing Department with one employee. The department's focus was on classical marketing activities, namely advertising campaigns (Illustration 1, "Marketing Department").[3] From its founding in 2003 through 2006, the Volksbank Serbia had no uniform, formal strategy for public relations (communications concepts for various target groups: employees, media, opinion leaders, shareholders, the

---

1 As can be seen from the following chapters, public relations at the Volksbank Serbia refers to reputation management and communication with various target groups: employees, media, shareholders, opinion leader and the general public.
2 Interview with Mag. Wöber, Director of Financial Strategy, Volksbank International AG
3 Cf. Interview with M. Ruzic, Director of Marketing and Communications Volksbank Serbia, p. 65

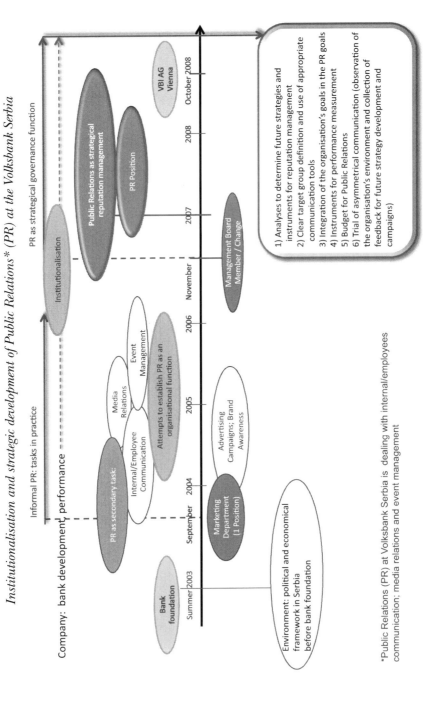

Illustration 1: Case study presented along the timeline – author's depiction

general public; (see Chapter 3.6) As shown in Illustration 1 and explained in Chapter 3 (Development Process of Public Relations 2003-2008), one employee who had other responsibilities within the bank was also responsible for PR tasks.

Thus from 2003 to 2006 public relations at the bank was carried out without an established post or strategy (Illustration 1, 2003-2006, presented in Chapter 3). Attempts to establish a separate public relations unit were repeatedly rejected by the Executive Board, who considered it unnecessary. Nevertheless public relations developed into a recognized unit at the Volksbank Serbia (Illustration 1, from 2007 public relations as strategic reputation management, institutionalisation of PR, discussed in detail in Chapter 3).

1 Initial situation

1.1 The environment: the nation

1.1.1 Serbia in 1999: Hunger, cold, inflation, unemployment

At the end of the 1990's the country's political state was chaotic and its economic state had hit rock bottom.[4] After the civil wars in former Yugoslavia from 1991 to 1997 and the NATO air strikes on Serbia in 1999 due to the war in Kosovo, Professor Oschlies of the Federal Institute for Eastern European Economy and International Studies wrote a summary of the regime of Slobodan Milosevic, at that time President of Serbia and Montenegro; in it he described the situation in Serbia in the winter of 1999/2000 as marked by "...*Hunger, cold, inflation, unemployment.*"[5] During the NATO air strikes from March through June 1999 the country suffered severe material damage – the weak economy was paralysed by EU and US sanctions during the war years and by the NATO intervention.[6]

---

4 Bertelsmann Stiftung, Serbia and Montenegro National Survey 2003, http://bti2003.bertelsmann-transformation-index.de/168.0.html – last checked on 23/08/2011

5 Economy and politics 1999 through 2000: "Serbia after Milosevic: Stability factors in South-eastern Europe", Prof. Dr. Wolf Oschlies, Research Associate of the Foundation for Economics and Politics, Berlin, www.bmlv.gv.at – last checked on 23/08/2011

6 Economy and politics 1999 through 2000: "Serbia after Milosevic: Stability factors in South-eastern Europe", Prof. Dr. Wolf Oschlies, Research Associate of the Foundation for Economics and Politics, Berlin, www.bmlv.gv.at – last checked on 23/08/2011

1.1.2. Political and economic turnaround: Serbia on the path to the EU

Political upheaval and democratisation of the country followed the downfall of Slobodan Milosevic's political party in October 2000 after violent demonstrations by the Serbian people on 5 October 2000, protesting electoral fraud.[7]

The new democratic government promised to clean things up: from 2001 through 2008 the country managed to begin the transformation process to a free market economy and to carry out significant structural reforms (liberalization of foreign trade, privatization of public property, reform of the banking industry and liberalization of the labour market).[8]

After the turnaround in 2000 Serbia opened itself to foreign investment and to cooperation with the EU. Austrian companies were and are the most important foreign investors in Serbia. The reform and opening up of the banking sector to the international market began in the years 2001 and 2002.[9] The nation found itself in a rapid transition from a centrally controlled command economy to a free market economy.

2 The organisation – development and strategy

2.1 Challenges to the newly founded bank in a nation in transition

The Volksbank Serbia was founded in an economically and politically difficult environment in September 2003 by the acquisition of a local bank, which dealt exclusively with corporate customers.[10] Two important condi-

---

7 Demonstrations on 5 October 2000: the front page of the periodical "Vreme"read "THE END"; the newspaper "Politika" published an article titled "Serbia on the path to democracy". During the demonstrations there were riots involving police and demonstrators during which the Parliament in the center of Belgrade was set on fire: Photos 8–10, p. 68
8 Chamber of Commerce of the Republic of Serbia: "The Serbian Economy" www.pks.rs – last checked on 20/08/2011; Appendix: p. 69–71; Macroeconomic Indicators 2001 through 2007; "Serbia Basic Economic Indicators", p. 72
9 Austria's Direct Investment Portfolio 2009 in Central and Eastern Europe, Austrian Chamber of Commerce www.wko.at – last checked on 23/08/2011, p. 73
10 Excerpt from the 2009 Annual Report of the Volksbank International AG, www.vbi.at – last checked on 23/08/.2011 and Appendix: p. 89

tions for market entry were the growth potential of the country itself with respect to the economy and the good investment climate.[11]

Before, the newly founded bank had neither dealt with private customers, nor did it have a network of branches. In 2003 the bank had 62 employees and one head office with 343 customers.[12] The mid- and long-term strategy of the Volksbank in Serbia was to achieve a market share of 5% and to be present in the big cities.[13]

To illustrate the bank's rapid growth, the development of the number of customers, employees and branches and the market share based on total assets from 2003 to 2008 are presented here:[14]

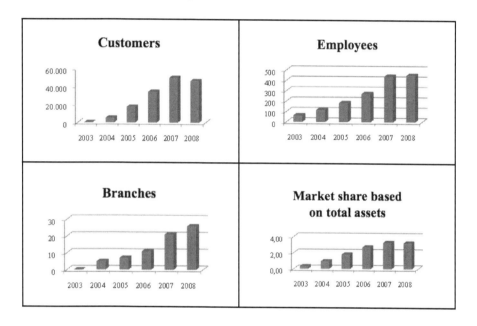

2.2 Conclusion: rapid growth = need for redirection

Comparison of the charts shows that the bank had developed quickly within five years. Due to increasing numbers of customers and employees (over

---

11 Cf. Interview with Mag. Wöber, Director of Financial Strategy Volksbank International AG, p. 64
12 Key figures of the Volksbank Serbia: Development 2003 through 2008, p. 90
13 Cf. Interview with Mag. Wöber, Director of Financial Strategy Volksbank International AG, p. 63
14 Performance figures of the Volksbank Serbia: Development 2003 through 2008, p. 90

50,000 customers and 420 employees in 2008), the network of branches was also expanded to 26, which necessitated an appropriate adjustment of the bank's organisational orientation. This included the Marketing Department; a PR position did not yet exist. This will be presented in detail in Chapter 3.

3 The path to institutionalised public relations in the Volksbank Serbia – what actually happened, and above all, how?

This section describes the circumstances and conditions existing in the period from 2003 to 2008 when the public relations unit of the bank was established and the actions, which contributed to the establishment of the post of Public Relations Manager after three years (presented in Chapter 3.8).[15] The focus is on the development of public relations as operations and activities in practice (organisational framework) and the career of the Public Relations Manager (personal framework).

3.1 From PR amateur to PR professional in a newly founded bank

This case deals with the question of how informal involvement with PR work as a secondary task in a bank becomes an organisationally anchored task, and more specifically, which actions contributed to the fact that, three years after it was founded, the Volksbank established PR as a strategic control function, and how the position of the Public Relations Manager came into existence when this had not been planned. "Informal involvement with PR" is taken here to mean that for three years all PR activities at the bank were carried out without a position having been established for the purpose. From 2003 to 2006 the Marketing Head worked alone in the department and explained, *"During this phase there was no position planned. Above all, no position in public relations was planned. Management had no grasp of PR at all. There was no consciousness on the management level of the necessity of this field of activity."*[16]

---

15 Illustration 1, Development of public relations work from 2003 to 2008, author's depiction
16 Interview with Maja Ruzic, Director of Marketing and Communications Volksbank Serbia, p. 65

After three years, public relations had fought its way into the company's organizational chart and was officially recognized in the bank (see Illustration 1, from 2007, institutionalisation of PR, presented in detail in Chapter 3.8).

Three important conditions contributed to the establishment by the Volksbank Serbia of a strategically planned unit and position for public relations:

1. The political and economic framework conditions and circumstances in Serbia – the country found itself in a rapid transition from a centrally controlled command economy to a free market economy; democratization of the country (described in Chapters 2.1 and 4.1)
2. The newly founded bank in a country in transition and the need for new instruments in reputation management and customer acquisition and retention due to strong competition in the banking sector (described in Chapters 2.2 and 4.2)
3. Individual development and motivation of one employee to establish this area of the bank organizationally, as well as results of PR work (described in Chapter 3 and summarised in Chapter 6).

3.2 After the bank was founded, the Marketing Department dealt with press relations as needed

As already mentioned in the first chapter, the Volksbank Serbia had a Marketing Department with one employee since it had been founded in 2003 (see Illustration 1). The concentration was on classical marketing activities, namely advertising campaigns.[17] The focus of the Marketing Department was brand awareness within the strategy of market entry and relatively solitary campaigns by the bank, as can be seen in the Marketing Strategy 2005: *"After the foundation of VBS in 2003, the main goal of the 2004 marketing activities was to establish the Volksbank brand on the Serbian market through institutional marketing. In addition, another aim was to support the sales efforts of the Retail and Corporate Divisions through product oriented marketing measures."*[18]

PR work was performed by the Marketing Department and was limited to activities with journalists, specifically to press conferences,[19] since, as can be

---

17 Cf. Interview with Maja Ruzic, Director of Marketing and Communications Volksbank Serbia, p. 65
18 Marketing Strategy 2005, p. 95
19 Marketing Strategy 2004, p. 103

seen from the Marketing Strategy 2004, press work was planned and realized at short notice: *"Press conferences [...] organised whenever needed for introduction of new services, results, activities, people, etc."*[20]

It can be seen that the Marketing Strategy in 2003 and 2004 includes no definition or goals for PR work. The connections between the organisation's goals and the "PR activities" (press conferences)[21] set forth in that strategy cannot be documented. The conclusion is that medium-term planning relating to reputation management, which is usually dealt with by Public Relations, was not possible.

3.3 PR activities become the secondary area of responsibility of the Assistant to the Executive Board

The area of PR was nevertheless allocated to the Assistant to the Executive Board: internal and employee communication, event management and intranet communication were brought to life and put into practice (in the Marketing Department's strategic planning this was first set down in 2007; see Chapter 3.1 and Illustration 1 – informal PR activity).[22]

The organization, however, had learned from its mistakes. Thus a chapter about "lessons learned in 2004" in the marketing strategy for 2005 mentions that many ad hoc decisions were made, which resulted in faulty implementation of good ideas: "*Ad Hoc Decision Making: our planning for 2005 is more detailed and strict than the 2004 plan, in order to reduce, as far as possible, the need for ad hoc decisions. In 2004, the high frequency of ad hoc decisions often resulted in bad implementation of a, fundamentally, good idea.*"[23]

3.4 Rapid growth in the bank, more need for public relations

The Volksbank expanded rapidly in 2005 (it already had more than 17,000 customers, 7 branches and 182 employees, as presented in Chapter 2.2.2), which resulted in strong competition for new customers and market share

---

20 Marketing Strategy 2004, p. 103
21 Marketing Strategy 2004, p. 103
22 PR Strategy 2007, Target Group Definition, p. 108
23 Marketing Strategy 2005, p. 96

among the banks.[24] The need for planned PR duties grew: proactive organization of press relations and targeted communications measures with other target groups – customers, business partners of the bank and shareholders.

As practice in 2005 showed, the bank employed more instruments for customer acquisition and retention and for positioning because the pressure of competition had increased (monthly customer events at the branches were organized; a business club for corporate customers was founded: lectures, workshops and networking events took place once per quarter; activities for employees were organized on a monthly basis, e.g. internal sales competitions for certain bank products, excursions and sports activities for employees; an employee club was founded with a designated budget and annual planning; proactive press work with planned themes and active communication with the press were realized: articles and interviews were published on a weekly basis).[25] It can be seen in Chapter 3 "*PR Activity in 05*"[26] of the marketing strategy for 2005 that qualitative and quantitative goals for press relations were set for the first time. Press relations became measurable and benefits could be determined.

3.5 First signs of organizational establishment: Important course setting on the path to institutionalisation of PR

In the marketing strategy for 2006, public relations activity within the Marketing Department was presented as organizationally separate from marketing activity (Illustration 2, highlighted.)[27] This action can be seen as a first indication of institutionalization and organizational establishment of public relations.

The benefits of PR in the previous year were recognized: a media resonance analysis[28] (quantitative: number of articles in the media, and qualitative: favourability of the articles) was carried out and recorded in this docu-

---

24 Excerpt from the records of the meeting of the Supervisory Board of the Volksbank Serbia on 02.12.2003: "Serbian Economy/ Banking Sector", p. 77–78
25 PR Calendar 2006: in the calendar activities which were carried out were listed by the PR Manager, p. 168–169; Employee Newsletter, overview 2005, p. 112–117; CV Natasa Ilic, p. 109
26 PR Strategy 2005, p. 130
27 Marketing Plan 2006, p. 159
28 Media resonance analysis is an instrument for efficiency monitoring and a method of evaluation for press clippings and articles and reports in the media.

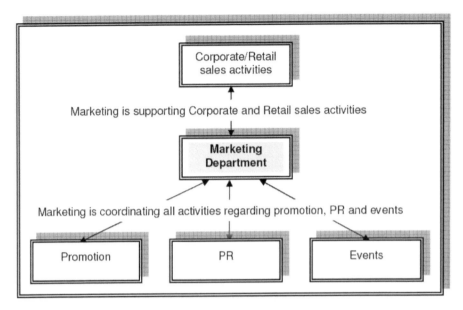

Illustration 2: PR activity is presented separately within the Marketing Department from "Marketing Plan 2006"

ment: *"PR activities were significantly improved in 2005; there were 412 published articles about Volksbank with the positive meaning and 20 minutes on TV stations."*[29]

From the author's point of view it is significant that in this document "events" and "promotion" are presented as separate from PR. In this context a discrepancy between planning and practice can be recognized: in practice events and promotional activities were carried out within public relations.[30] The Assistant to the Executive Board was responsible for these tasks[31] (PR, events and promotion) but this is not explicitly stated in the marketing strategy for 2006.[32]

It can be seen that the bank concentrated on events in its branches.[33] The Volksbank's branches were positioned in the pedestrian zones of Belgrade,

---

29 Marketing Plan 2006, p. 165
30 PR Calendar 2006: in the calendar activities, which were carried out, were listed by the PR Manager, p. 168–169
31 Invitation to the event, organization, preparations, communication with the media and the media response, p. 173–185
32 Marketing Plan 2006, p. 159
33 Marketing Plan 2006, p. 165

the capital of Serbia, and in its other large cities (Novi Sad, Subotica, Cacak, Nis) and were therefore well suited for events.[34] By carrying out these events[35] the bank focused on attracting the attention of the public.[36] The result was extensive media reports.[37] In 2006 a business club for business partners and corporate customers of the bank was founded.[38] The business club organized lectures on current topics several times a year for corporate customers. As shown in practice, the year 2006 was marked by numerous events for various target groups (media, customers, employees, business partners).[39] In the marketing strategy for 2006, activities for employees were focused on an internal sales competition. As can be seen from practice, however, the employee club organized a number of events.[40] The Assistant to the Executive Board was responsible for all these activities.[41]

The conclusion is that public relations had unofficially established itself within the Marketing Department. As shown in Illustration 2, PR was separated from events and promotion. In practice, however, there was evidence of a uniform accomplishment of PR, events and promotion.

From the author's point of view the discrepancy between marketing strategy and practice can be traced back to an incomplete definition of the concept of public relations and the organizational assignment of tasks in the Marketing Department (What is to be done? Who does what? What is the

---

34 Volksbank Serbia branch network – www.volksbank.rs, last checked on 25.08.2011
35 Wellness Day events were organized to take place in four cities on the same day: on Women's Day, 8 March (this date was and is celebrated in Serbia) ladies were invited to come to the bank's branches, where they could get advice from professional cosmetologists on skin care, as well as have their makeup done. Prominent singers and emcees took part in the events. Invitation to the event on 8 March, p. 170–171; the media reported accordingly
36 Volksbank NEWS – employee newsletter: overview 2006, p. 118–120
37 The national television broadcaster RTS reports intensively (4'45") in a program on 25.04.2006, recording available on DVD
38 Marketing Strategy 2006, p. 163
39 Following positive experience the previous year, the Easter Festival was organized to take place in five cities for the second time: Volksbank NEWS – employee newsletter: overview 2006, p. 120, photos Nr. 77-79, p. 173, Invitation, organization in detail p. 174-179, media response p. 180-183, Auction of Volksbank Easter eggs at a museum in Belgrade (the money raised was donated to an orphanage), p. 184, further events: photos Nr. 82-84 "First day of school with the Volksbank", p. 185
40 Volksbank NEWS – employee newsletter: overview 2006, p. 118–120
41 Business Club 2006, "Workshop for the management" organization and process, p. 172

goal? What is the plan? Are resources available – budget, employees? Is the plan realized? What can be learned for the future?)

3.6 Actions resulting from practice and results of PR work led to the birth of a new organizational area

The inference by summarizing Chapters 3.1 through 3.5 is that for three years, beginning from its founding in 2003, the Volksbank Serbia has had no uniform, formal strategy for PR work (communications concepts for various target groups: employees, media, opinion leaders, shareholders, the general public). Nevertheless, an employee (the Assistant to the Executive Board, later employed in the HR Department) took responsibility for PR tasks although she had other tasks within the bank (shown in Illustration 1). 2003 the Assistant to the Executive Board took over in succession the tasks of internal and employee communication, press relations and events management and carried these out until the end of 2006 (see Illustration 1, development of PR work from 2003 through 2008).

PR work in the bank took place, therefore, without an existing position and strategy. Attempts to establish a separate public relations position or unit were repeatedly rejected by the Executive Board, who considered it unnecessary. Since public relations was not a priority at the Volksbank, a position in the Marketing Department was not planned during the bank's first three years.[42] The Marketing Head of Volksbank Serbia at that time said in an interview that the bank management had no grasp of the necessity of this field of activity.[43]

The conclusion is that after its founding the Volksbank recognized the necessity for and benefits of a reciprocal flow of communication with its target groups. In the first step, in 2003 and 2004, communication with employees (as presented in Chapter 3.3.) was established through the foundation of an employee club[44] with regular events, the publication of an employee newsletter[45] and the opening of an intranet portal. In a further step,

---

42 Cf. Interview with Maja Ruzic, Director of Marketing and Communications Volksbank Serbia, p. 65
43 Cf. Interview with Maja Ruzic, Director of Marketing and Communications Volksbank Serbia, p. 65
44 Founding of Sports & Fun Club, p. 110–111, Budget and Program for the events for employees in 2005, p. 144
45 Volksbank NEWS – employee newsletter Overview 2005/2006/2007, p. 112–125

in 2005 and 2006, proactive media work took place with regular press conferences[46] and round tables with journalists. To reach customers and the general public, monthly events in the branches were organized.[47]

3.7 Changes in the Executive Board bring new perspectives for the institutionalisation of PR

In autumn 2006 a new Executive Board Member (CEO) for the Volksbank Serbia was announced. The majority owner, the Volksbank International AG in Vienna, decided on this change in September 2006. Thus at the end of October 2006 the Executive Board member who was responsible for the Assistant to the Executive Board and Public Relations/Marketing left the Volksbank.[48]

In her closing appraisal interview with the Board Member, the Assistant pointed out once again the need for a position for public relations. She presented the results of the previous three years (goals had been reached and exceeded, as presented in Chapter 3.4 and 3.10, if PR work were measured) and emphasized that the workload in her double role could no longer be carried out. Her request for a transfer to the Marketing Department was refused.[49]

The Assistant to the Executive Board remembers the autumn of 2006 as follows: *"To this day I do not know whether the real reason was that no position existed/was planned/was budgeted for. The need for a position had been established through the results of the previous three years. The bank had grown. One person in the Marketing Department of a bank with more than 11 branches and more than 270 employees was too little, not only in my opinion but also in the opinion of the Marketing Director at that time. As a 'reward' for my work and success in the previous three years I was offered a position in the Human Resources Department. The main focus of my tasks was project work in the area of personnel. The Public Relations agenda was to be maintained as my secondary field of responsibility."*[50]

The employee worked in the Human Resources Department for two months. PR activities remained her responsibility.

---

46 Photos Nr. 41–43 from the press conference at World Savings Day, p. 136; media reports by the television broadcaster RTS, Novi Sad, BK, p. 132–135
47 Invitation to the Easter celebration, to do list, p. 141–142; photos Nr. 53–55 from the events in branches, p. 143
48 http://www.volksbank.rs/izvrsni-upravni-odbor – last checked on 20.08.2011
49 Journal, Natasa Ilic, p. 260
50 Journal Natasa Ilic, p. 260

In November 2006 the Volksbank Serbia got a new Executive Board Chairman – Axel Hummel, who is still to this day Chief Executive Officer (CEO) of the Volksbank Serbia.[51] The task of the unofficial Public Relations Manager in the Human Resources Department was to introduce the new Executive Board Chairman and the bank's strategy for the year 2007 to the media. For this purpose a press conference was called at the beginning of 2007. The press conference was attended by the elite among the business journalists.[52]

The unofficial PR Manager and employee of the Human Resources Department: *"I was very happy that the new Executive Board Chairman had entrusted me with this press conference. He did not know me; I worked in the Human Resources Department. All of the communication, presentation and enquiries by the journalists were my responsibility. I was in a good position to talk about my future with the bank. This gave me hope at last that I should not leave the Volksbank! I saw my chance. After all, I did not want to simply give up what had been built up in the Volksbank in the last three years."*[53]

3.8 The position of Public Relations Manager was approved: the employee's interests met the bank's needs

The employee who had carried out the PR activities for almost three years while holding down another job in the bank was officially transferred to the position of Public Relations Manager in the Marketing Department by resolution of the Executive Board on 14th January 2007.[54] The position was approved. The Department was soon renamed "Marketing and Communications". The job description was written by the Public Relations Manager.[55] The Head of Marketing, Maja Ruzic, said in an interview: *"The change in management resulted in different circumstances. In this sense there were no more limits for Ms. Ilic. She has already performed the tasks for almost three years. We assumed that the results of PR work would be better after Ms. Ilic was able to devote herself 100% to this task!"*[56]

---

51 Axel Hummel, CEO - http://www.volksbank.rs/izvrsni-upravni-odbor – last checked on 20.08.2011
52 Article in the periodical "VREME", p. 201 (Interview with Axel Hummel); photos Nr. 92–93, p. 211
53 Journal Natasa Ilic, p. 260
54 Resolution of the Executive Board "Executive Board decision Natasa Ilic", p. 212
55 Job description PR Manager, p. 62
56 Interview with M. Ruzic, Director of Marketing and Communications Volksbank Serbia, p. 66

Ultimately, due to the change in the Executive Board the need for an organizationally defined area of public relations was recognized. Documents such as the job description, goals for PR work, performances measurement, media resonance analysis, reporting to the Executive Board, strategy and budget for PR and integration of PR goals in the organizational goals were introduced.[57]

3.9 Individual development and motivation of an employee and results of the informally carried out PR work

As described in Chapters 3.1 to 3.8, an employee had taken on the tasks of PR work as a secondary field, learned from this practice and had done extra-occupational training.[58]

The conclusion is that the standards of PR work in the bank which the PR Manager had introduced and determined, the job description, strategy and goals for all activities are all still valid in the Volksbank Serbia today (The Public Relations Manager of the Volksbank Serbia has been employed by the Volksbank International AG, the holding company in Vienna, since October 2008.[59]).

In this connection the statement as to what characterizes a successful PR Manager will be argued from the point of view of the Public Relations Manager (personal context of the case). In the experience of the Public Relations Manager in the case described here, the crucial factor for professional success (in combination with appropriate experience and education) is that the person takes pleasure in her job and keeps her eyes on the goal. The vision of this employee at the beginning of her banking career was to become PR Manager of the bank.[60] The Public Relations Manager says: *"Today I can say that at that time I had real luck. Perhaps it was beginner's luck. I simply trusted my gut instinct. The ideas came one after the other and I knew how to realize*

---

57 PR Strategy 2007, p. 107–108; PR Budget 2007, p. 213; Marketing and Communications Plan-VB Serbia, p. 214; Report to the Executive Board, p. 215–218; Budget Control: number of PR announcements, p. 216- 217; Employee Performance Appraisal Natasa Ilic 6M 2008, p. 219– 220

58 Diploma, University Megatrend, Faculty for Culture and Media, Belgrade, Serbia, p. 187

59 Cf. Interview with M. Ruzic, Director of Marketing and Communications Volksbank Serbia, p. 65

60 Journal Natasa Ilic, p. 256

them, but it was not a conscious process. Today I would examine, develop and analyse strategies, work out a number of scenarios and reckon with this or that problem or barrier, plan for risks–but I would always trust my gut instinct. Today I ask myself the central question: Which mix of knowledge and education, experience and gut instinct is crucial for a Public Relations Manager? In my experience, the mix is 60% trust in one's own gut instinct and pleasure in doing the work. The remaining 40% is practical experience and education. Trust is therefore essential; trust that things will go well if they are done from the heart and with joy. And for five years I have always performed my PR tasks from my heart, with much love and joy. I had my vision and remained true to it. From my point of view, that is what makes a PR professional."[61]

3.10 Public Relations as a control function and reputation management: strategic focus of PR in the Volksbank since the end of 2006

In the following two years (2007 and 2008) an integrated Marketing and Communications plan with quantitative and qualitative goals for PR was determined.[62] The goals set were exceeded in both years.[63]

From the strategies for 2007 and 2008 it can be seen that communications campaigns in parallel to and in support of marketing campaigns in the bank were planned and became an integrated component of the Marketing and Communications strategy. A separate budget for PR activities was assured.[64] The Public Relations Manager was responsible for the creation of the communication strategy and the budget, which from 2007 onwards was a detailed document separate from the marketing plan.[65]

Documents, such as quarterly and annual reports to the Executive Board on the results of PR as well as reports on media coverage of the competition

---

61 Journal Natasa Ilic, p. 262
62 PR Strategy 2007 and PR Budget 2007, p. 108; Annual Report of the Volksbank Serbia 2007 – www.volksbank.rs, last checked on 16/08/2011 and Appendix/Source documents: Excerpt from the Annual Report, p. 32; Volksbank Investment Centre Campaign 2008, p. 221–224; Volksbank PR Print value, p. 218 and Report to the Executive Board of the Volksbank Serbia on the results of 2007, submitted by the Public Relations Manager, discussed at the Board meeting on 16/01/2008, p. 215
63 Budget Control: number of PR announcements, p. 216– 217; Employee Performance Appraisal Natasa Ilic 6M 2008, p. 219–220
64 PR Strategy 2007 and PR Budget 2007, p. 108
65 PR Strategy 2007, p. 107–108; PR Budget 2007, p. 213; Marketing and Communications Plan-VB Serbia, p. 214

The path to institutionalised public relations in the Volksbank Serbia

Number of PR announcements

	2004			2005			2006			2007			2008		
	Positive	Total	% of Positive	Positive	Total	% of Positive	Positive	Total	% of Positive	Positive	Total	% of Positive	Positive	Total	% of Positive
January	3	4	75%	3	7	43%	7	29	24%	11	21	52%	10	22	45%
February	1	14	7%	20	49	41%	14	37	38%	46	56	82%	19	53	36%
March	9	12	75%	32	60	53%	16	58	28%	31	56	55%	32	63	51%
April	14	16	88%	11	35	31%	16	46	35%	25	43	58%	33	74	45%
May	6	15	40%	7	30	23%	7	37	19%	12	37	32%	33	67	49%
June	9	24	38%	10	23	43%	6	36	17%	22	45	49%	39	56	70%
July	9	16	56%	4	22	18%	11	19	58%	18	33	55%	35	53	66%
August	2	11	18%	19	51	37%	12	24	50%	17	28	61%	11	26	42%
September	7	18	39%	12	30	40%	21	37	57%	25	51	49%	41	72	57%
October	2	14	14%	13	40	33%	32	49	65%	44	77	57%	51	101	50%
November	2	19	11%	12	53	23%	12	24	50%	35	70	50%	36	70	51%
December	4	13	31%	8	23	35%	7	28	25%	20	38	53%	40	64	63%
TOTAL:	68	176	39%	151	417	36%	161	424	38%	315	560	56%	380	721	53%
Increase in % yoy					137%			2%			32%			29%	

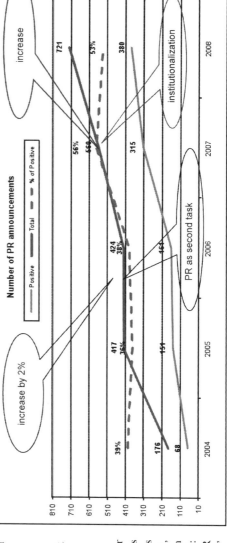

Illustration 3: Number of published articles and contributions in the media from 2004 to 2008, from "Budget Control: number of PR announcements"

Illustration 4: Number of published articles and contributions 2004 to 2008, diagrammed, from "Budget Control: number of PR announcements"

153

were introduced starting in 2007 and became regular practice in the bank.[66] Instruments of performance measurement, such as media resonance analysis, were presented to the full Board in quarterly reports. One part of these reports is presented in Illustration 3: in the column labelled "Total" in the table is the total number of articles and contributions about the bank which appeared in print and electronic media in the period 2004-2008. The number and corresponding percentage of the reports which were positive (positive means with a positive mark or opinion of the bank by the journalist) are presented in the column labelled "Positive".[67]

The contributions in the media climbed from 176 in 2004 to 721 in 2008 (highlighted in Illustration 4). Total contributions in 2007 rose by 32% in comparison to the previous year; in 2006 the increase in comparison to 2005 was only 2% (see Illustration 4, commentary).

It is interesting to see that with the introduction of a PR position the percentage of positive contributions exceeded 50%, which had been set as a goal in 2005; in 2007 it were 56% but in 2006 only 38%. By this instrument the quantitative work of the Public Relations Manager was measured.

Public Relations Manager: *"Further analyses were carried out to make planning of PR work more efficient. Equivalence analysis or advertising equivalence is a method which converts article length into advertising cost, i.e. it calculates what these articles would cost if they were paid for as advertising."*[68]

According to analysis by the clipping agency Ninamedia in Belgrade, the value of the 721 press articles in 2008 was €270,985 and in 2007 €225,900 – excluding taxes and contributions in electronic media.[69] With classical advertising the sum of more than €500,000 would have had to be invested in the two years. Public relations had spent 4% of the total marketing budget (average per year).[70] At this point a clear benefit of PR work can be recognized (Note: these analyses were first carried out in 2007). The analyses presented have been carried out regularly in the Volksbank Serbia since 2007.

A performance appraisal of the Public Relations Manager took place twice a year.[71] For the first time employee satisfaction with internal activities

---

66 Report to the Executive Board, p. 215–218
67 Budget Control: number of PR announcements, p. 216–217
68 Journal Natasa Ilic, p. 261
69 Volksbank PR Print value, p. 218 and Report to the Executive Board of the Volksbank Serbia on the Results for 2007, submitted by the Public Relations Manager, discussed at the Executive Board meeting on 16/01/.2008, p. 215
70 Report to the Executive Board, p. 215
71 Employee Performance Appraisal Natasa Ilic 6M 2008, p. 219–220

(information flow, intranet design, newsletter, events) was surveyed.[72] Media coverage of the competition was followed and the topics analysed. Tracking of topics was adopted as an early warning system.[73] Thus the bank planned and steered its communication with various target groups and when necessary, for example in crises, it could intervene in time. From the author's point of view this constitutes a basis for reputation management.

The Public Relations Manager explained that this control function and the analyses were important for medium- and long-term planning of PR activities: *"Because, as Peter Drucker says, 'If you can't measure it, you can't manage it.'"*[74]

As can be seen from the case study, strategically planned and controlled work took place. Strategically controlled PR work at the Volksbank Serbia in 2007 and 2008 is described as such based on the following six points:

1. a wide range and variety of communication channels between the bank and its target groups; clear target group definition and use of appropriate communication tools
2. integration of the organisation's goals in the PR goals (Chapter 3.10.)
3. budget for Public Relations[75]
4. instruments for performance measurement, regular reporting to the Executive Board (as described in Chapter 3.10, Illustrations 3 and 4)
5. analyses to determine future strategies and instruments for reputation management (Chapter 3.10)
6. trial of asymmetrical communication (observation of the organisation's environment and collection of feedback – described in Chapter 3.10) with the general public[76]

It can be seen that strategically controlled public relations work at the Volksbank Serbia took place in 2007, as this was organizationally incorporated into the organization as a reputation management function.

---

72 Employee Performance Appraisal Natasa Ilic 6M 2008, p. 219– 220
73 PR Strategy 2007 and PR Budget 2007, p. 107–108
74 Journal Natasa Ilic, p. 261
75 PR Strategy 2007, p. 107
76 Annual Report of the Volksbank Serbia 2007 – www.volksbank.rs, last checked on 16/08/2011 and Appendix/Source documents: Excerpt from the Annual Report, p. 32

4 Theoretical embedding

Theoretical approaches will be used in the following to examine what, from the point of view of theory and in connection with the case, characterizes strategic PR work, and accordingly, when and under what conditions (actions and organizational changes) and circumstances (market conditions) it happens and is successfully realized in practice.

The research question of how informal dealings with PR can become institutionalised professional activity is observed from a theoretical point of view within the following two contexts:

a) In the context of the nation of Serbia (socio-political development of the country)
b) In the context of the organisation (the bank and PR work as task, actions, function)

Ad a) for the research of the phenomenon/the research question in the context of the nation of Serbia (geopolitical development of the country, Chapter 2.1), social theoretical approaches will be used in Chapter 4.1.

Ad b) for the research of the phenomenon/the research question in the context of the organization, organizational theories will be used (Chapter 4.2). Here the point of view of the organization will be used, and the integration process of public relations as an organizational component in a bank will be presented in theory (the case in organizational context).

In the first step the social theoretical approaches of Ronneberger and Rühl were used (context: nation of Serbia – socio-political development of the country) to examine the influences of the environment. In the next step the organizational theoretical approaches of Grunig and Hunt are presented (context: the organization – the bank and PR work as task, actions, function).

4.1 Social theories: modern society and competition as conditions for professional PR work

The goal here was to research, which social framework conditions are necessary for the development of public relations and on what level public relations is carried out as function and action/activity with respect to the entire society (see the case section "The Nation", Chapter 2.1). In the framework of social theories, Ronneberger and Rühl explain which circumstances and conditions must be present in a country/market for the establishment of public relations as an organizational field in an organization (macro, meso and micro levels).[77]

From the point of view of social theory approaches, the basis for PR is modern society as a welfare society.[78] In connection with the political and economic changes in Serbia (macro level), the society had developed to the point (rapid transition in Serbia as described in Chapter 2.1) where public relations could be recognized as a necessity (increasing competition and rapid expansion in the bank, as presented in Chapter 2.2).

4.2 Organization theories: PR as a central function is an achievement of organizational goals

The next step here is to apply organization theories in context of the organization.[79] The point of view of the organization theory developed by Grunig and Hunt considers the achievement of organizational goals (what is of benefit for the organization) as a central PR function.[80] As in the case presented in Chapter 3, PR work in the three years following the bank's founding in 2003 was allocated to one employee as a secondary area of responsibility. At this point it can be inferred that the benefit of Public Relations in these three years was recognized because an employee had attended to the tasks. It was determined, however, that it was not until the introduction of instruments of performance measurement in 2007 that the quantitative benefit for the organization was calculated. The conclusion from the case described here is that strategically controlled, formal PR took place after the establishment of a PR position in the Volksbank.

The theories presented in Chapters 4.1 and 4.2 lead to the insight that the social theoretical approaches of Ronneberger and Rühl, as well as the organization theories of Grunig and Hunt clearly answer the question of how informal dealings with PR can become institutionalized professional activity. The next step is a successful definition of what professional PR activity means:

---

77 Cf. Ronneberger/Rühl (1992): Public Relations. A draft quoted by Szyszka, Peter (2004): PR work as organisational function, p. 151
78 Cf. Ronneberger/Rühl, Theory of Public Relations. A draft, presentation, p. 265
79 Grunig / Hunt 1984, p. 6
80 Model of PR according to Grunig and Hunt (1984); Rötger (2000), p. 45; Signitzer 2004, p. 157

"Professional PR activity in an organisation can be described as such and can then take place when the social framework conditions are met (modern society/market economy and competition), the need for this activity in the organisation is recognized (qualitative and quantitative analyses, instruments of performance measurement in order to control reputation management and develop strategies) and a commensurate position, job description, goal setting and integration into the organisation's goals are present."[81] Following this definition it must be emphasized that professional PR work is present when it is institutionalized and organizationally and strategically anchored in the organization.

4.3 Definitions of the public, communication and public relations

The concluding chapter about the theoretical approaches deals with the concepts of the public, communication and public relations. Since the bank was constantly a focal point for the public (the public = employees, media, shareholders, customers) it needed communication with its public or target groups, since attention is attracted not only by active communication but also by the behaviour of an organization.[82]

In the last section on theoretical embedding, various definitions of public relations are examined. By linking incidents from practice with parts of various definitions of PR from the theories, a definition of public relations at the Volksbank Serbia was successfully determined.[83]

"Public relations in the Volksbank Serbia is a distinctive management function (Harlow) which plans (Grunig) and realizes (Szyska) communication between the bank and its target groups with the goal of controlling the bank's reputation management in order to make a sustainable contribution to the achievement of the bank's objectives (PRVA)."[84]

In connection with the insights from the theories, in the following steps two scenarios from the case were presented and the consequences were examined.

---

81 Author's definition
82 Cf. Watzlawick, Paul/Beavin, Janet H./Jackson Don D. (1996): Human Communication, p. 53
83 Author's definition
84 Author's definition, derived from the theories presented

5 Scenarios of the case

5.1 Scenario 1: The tasks of the Marketing and Communications Department grow further and change

What happens if the bank is sold to an international player on the market?

The bank is sold to a major international bank. This major bank is new and unknown on the Serbian market. The new owner prepares a one-year image campaign, and in the preparation phase the Marketing and Communications Department is reorganized. The decision is made to divide the Marketing and Communications Department. Public Relations receives its own box in the organogram and two further employees are hired for this department. One of the jobs is Director of the Communications Department and two further jobs for internal communication and press relations are established. In cooperation with the Marketing Director, the PR Director creates a short- and medium-term communications plan on the subject of rebranding and repositioning for the new owner's market entry.

Consequences for PR: this scenario represents progress for the PR Department. Groundwork is laid to expand the PR strategy by at least two further segments: corporate and social responsibility and social media/online PR (as of the date of this publication the bank has not yet dealt with this subject). A further segment is public affairs or relationship management.

Consequences for the organization: due to this new PR strategy the bank assures its future reputation management and is prepared for times of crisis. New employees are hired and the organization grows.

5.2 Scenario 2: The importance of professional communication decreases

How could the importance of the Communications Department be lost again?

In the second scenario the bank suffers loan defaults of around 43% due to granting of high-risk loans (almost every second customer cannot pay his instalments). Due to changes in the law, however, new, stricter corporate actions are required. On the one hand the bank is deep in the red and on the other hand it urgently needs fresh capital. First of all, the bank's Executive Board decides on economy measures and closes five branches. The Marketing and Communications Department shrinks from three employees to one (only the Marketing Director remains) and both the PR job and the budget for PR activities are cut.

The first negative consequence is a shrinking media resonance because no one is dealing proactively with press relations any longer (lack of resources, budget). After a certain time the negative headlines in the media become even louder because the bank has no communications strategy for times of crisis and the bank's Executive Board suffers severe damage to its reputation (a long-term higher risk factor!), which can be attributed to inadequate management of crisis communication. The bank's customers are already alarmed and begin to withdraw their savings. The competition recognizes the bank's tilt early on and acquires customers with tempting offers. Because there are no resources available, the employee club is closed and no events take place. The mood among the employees is bad; they are living with uncertainty, fear of the future and fear of losing their jobs. The rumour mill is in full spin. The employees learn the bad news about the bank by the newspapers. Ultimately these actions lead to resignations among middle management. The bank loses 50% of its middle management and 30% of its customers.[85]

6 Summary of interpretation and conclusions

With reference to the specified research question of how informal dealings with PR can become institutionalized professional activity, it can be determined that the professional PR activity in the bank became possible due to the structural changes in the organization (Public Relations position) and took place as a result of market conditions (economic development and strong competition).

The insights from the case study (described in Chapter 3) together with the conclusions from the theories in the context of the case (presented in Chapters 4.1 through 4.3) and the consequences from the scenarios (as described in Chapters 5.1 and 5.2) confirm the author's definition of professional PR work:

"Professional PR activity in an organisation can be described as such and can then take place when the social framework conditions are met (modern society/market

---

[85] N.B. Author's explanatory note: this is only a scenario which I invented! Today the Volksbank Serbia is among the top ten of 33 banks on the market, with 450 employees, over 50,000 customers and 26 branches.

economy and competition), the need for this activity in the organisation is recognized (qualitative and quantitative analyses, instruments of performance measurement in order to control reputation management and develop strategies) and a commensurate position, job description, goal setting and integration into the organisation's goals are present.[86]

Whether and to what extent one employee contributed through her vision, motivation and commitment to the Volksbank Serbia's acquisition of institutionalized and strategically managed public relations cannot be scientifically proved in this article, but the case study described permits the assumption.

References

Books:

Grunig, James/Todd, Hunt (1984), Managing Public Relations. Holt, Rinehart and Winston, New York.
Ronneberger, Franz/Manfred Rühl (1992), Theorie der Public Relations. Ein Entwurf. Westdeutscher Verlag, Opladen.
Röttger, Ulrike (2000), Public Relations – Organisation und Profession. Öffentlichkeitsarbeit als Organisationsfunktion. Eine Berufsfeldstudie. Westdeutscher Verlag, Wiesbaden.
Signitzer, Benno (2004), Theorie der Public Relations. In: Burkart/Roland/Hömberg (2007), Kommunikationstheorien. Ein Textbuch zur Einführung. Vol. 8, 4th extended and updated edition, Braumüller, Wien.
Szyszka, Peter (1999), Public Relations und Öffentlichkeitsarbeit. Einführung in die Grundlagen. Skript zur Seminararbeit für Grundlagen der Organisationskommunikation am Institut für Kommunikations-Management, Lingen.
Szyszka, Peter (2004), PR Arbeit als Organisationsfunktion. Konturen eines organisationalen Theorieentwurfs zu Public Relations und Kommunikations-Management. In: Theorien der Public Relations. Grundlagen und Perspektiven der PR-Forschung. Ed.: Ulrike Röttger. VS Verlag für Sozialwissenschaften, Wiesbaden.
Szyszka, Peter (Dezember 1999), Grundzüge der Öffentlichkeitsarbeit. Skript im Rahmen der Seminararbeit am Institut für Kommunikations-Management, Offenburg/Lingen.
Watzlawick, Paul/Beavin, Janet H./Jackson Don D. (1996), Menschliche Kommunikation. Formen, Störungen, Paradoxien. 9th unchanged edition, Verlag Hans Huber, Bern, Göttingen, Toronto, Seattle.
Zerfaß, Ansgar (2004), Unternehmensführung und Öffentlichkeitsarbeit: Grundlegung einer Theorie der Unternehmenskommunikation und Public Relations. Verlag für Sozialwissenschaften, Wiesbaden.

Internet:

http://www.integrationsfonds.at/de/publikationen/laenderinformation/Serbia/ – last checked on 26.08.2011

http://www.bmlv.gv.at/wissen-forschung/publikationen/beitrag.php?id=226 – last checked on 26.08.2011

www.volksbank.rs – last checked on 25.08.2011

http://bti2003.bertelsmann-transformation-index.de/168.0.html - last checked on 23.08.2011

---

86 Author's definition

www.bmlv.gv.at – last checked on 23.08.2011

www.vbi.at – last checked on 23.08.2011

www.wko.at – last checked on 23.08.2011

http://www.volksbank.rs/izvrsni-upravni-odbor – last checked on 20.08.2011

www.pks.rs - last checked on 20.08.2011

http://www.prva.at/ueber-uns/grundlagen/leitbild/ - last checked on 05.08.2011

Empirical sources:

Interview with Mag. Gerhard Wöber, Director of Financial Strategy at the Volksbank International AG in Vienna, interview conducted in March 2011 in the offices of the Volksbank International in Vienna

Interview with Maja Ruzic, former Director of Marketing and Communications at the Volksbank Serbia (today Director of the Product Development and Sales Support Department at the Volksbank Serbia), Interview conducted in March 2011 in the offices of the Volksbank Serbia in Belgrade

Journal Natasa Ilic, former Public Relations Manager at the Volksbank Serbia – Original journal as source document

List of illustrations:

Illustration 1: Case study presented along the timeline – author's depiction

Illustration 2: PR activity is presented separately within the Marketing Department, from "Marketing Plan 2006"

Illustration 3: Illustration 3: Number of published articles and contributions in the media from 2004 to 2008, from "Budget Control: number of PR announcements"

Illustration 4: Illustration 4: Number of published articles and contributions 2004 to 2008, diagrammed, from "Budget Control: number of PR announcements"

Eva Maria Bauer

From individual learning to organisational learning

1 Introduction

This article discusses the question of whether both individual and organisational learning can be achieved through the composition of a case study. On the basis of episodic, guideline-supported interviews[1] with the four authors who made their case studies available in the form of articles for this book, their experiences during the composition of their case studies are documented. Subsequently the resulting insights on the subject of individual and organisational learning from the case study are summarized, discussed and interpreted.

The names and precise functions of the interview partners are replaced by the abbreviations IP 1 through IP 4. The length of each interview was between twenty and forty minutes. The interviews were recorded and transcribed. The evaluation of the interviews was carried out on the basis of Mayring's qualitative content analysis, which works with individual, previously determined steps of interpretation.[2]

The presentation of the results comprises the areas of individual and organisational learning.

The insights into individual learning are generated by the subjects:
1. Choice of topic
2. Composition of the case study with focus on its challenges

The insights into organisational learning are generated by the subjects:
1. Including one's own organisation when choosing the topic
2. Support from the organisation during the composition
3. Reactions to and learning from the case study by the organisation

According to the book *Research Case Studies as Learning Challenges for Leaders and Organisations*, above all learning should be generated as to how managers and their organisations can recognize and endorse learning through the composition of a thesis based on a case study.

---
1 Lamnek (2005), p. 363
2 Mayring (2010), p. 59

2 Presentation of results

2.1 Insights into individual learning

2.1.1 The first step of individual learning – choosing a topic

The interviews show that an important first step for the composition of a case study is finding a topic, which fulfils three important conditions: 1. It should be a time-limited case (for example, a process, a project in the organisation) from the author's own organisation or one which is well known to him or her. 2. Despite closeness to the topic, the author should be able to maintain emotional distance in order to describe the case objectively and non-judgmentally from the role of an observer. 3. Further, sufficient empirical material for the case description must be available to the observer.

All of the people who were interviewed chose cases from their direct working environment. The following points were important to the authors in their choices:

- Generation of insights from which profit could be derived and/or the reasons for success could be determined (IP 4)
- Strong identification with the topic (IP 2)
- Being a stakeholder in the case (IP 3)

As it turned out, the choice of topic was not easy, because it was a tightrope walk between personal identification with the case and sufficient emotional distance to permit an objective description of the case from an observer's role. Thus one author (IP 2) chose to make the organisation and key players anonymous in order to be able to describe the case objectively.

> IP 2: *"For me it was crucial to find a topic with which on the one hand I could personally identify, that is, to a certain degree to have been a part of the case or to have had insights into the topic. On the other hand it was also always very important not to be too emotionally caught up in the topic. This tightrope walk was certainly not always simple because I was a part of the subject. Nevertheless it was crucial for me as a next step to work on the topic again both for myself and for science and thus to have a bird's-eye view of certain points in which I was involved. One important part of this was certainly that from the beginning I made both the organisation and the people involved anonymous, so that I was more or less a third party. And thus it was possible for me to reduce this emotional attachment."*[3]

---

3 IP 2: Interview 2011, p. 1

When a case is found which fulfils the criteria, the result is greater challenges and opportunities for learning if it can be drawn on for a case study. Further, the interview partners achieved an awareness of how deeply they were linked to the case.

2.1.2 The path to the actual topic – support from the organisation

Choice of subject was the exclusive province of the author of the case study; consent from the decision-makers in the organisations was not secured until shortly before the final choice of topic (IP 1). The support the authors received from the organisations included permission to use material as evidence and the availability of key players and decision-makers for interviews (IP 2, IP 3, IP 4).

> IP 4: *"I chose my topic alone and then received permission to use research material and conduct interviews, for example with my supervisor."*[4]

It can be clearly seen that all organisations from which the cases stem knew about the authors' projects and gave their approval. Thus every organisation in its way made room for learning. A tendency to be open to organisational learning is evident both in the permission for the case study to be written and in the support provided through access to empirical material and interview partners.

2.1.3 A practical case becomes academic – structuring as a task

The composition of a case study is challenging after one has been professionally active for a number of years, since one is no longer directly involved with the academic preparation of texts. Further, a case study is constructed differently than many other academic papers. Each of the four authors had hurdles to overcome.

IP 1 emphasised that writing a case study is different to writing other academic papers because one begins with the practical part. So IP 1 tried to tell the reader a story and make it readable. Moreover, he paid careful attention

---

4   IP 4: Interview 2011, p. 1

to what the beginning and the end were and where there were provable milestones in the development and growth of the organisation.

IP 4, for example, simply started writing and did not even do any research. In the course of the writing, then, it became clear that it is absolutely necessary to have material and to be able to dig deeply into it. So IP 4 also recognized that first the research is important in order to have an impression of whether one has sufficient material so that one can proceed in a structured fashion. IP 4 experienced that structure is of primary importance.

IP 2 and IP 3 had similar experiences to IP 1 and IP 4. Therefore they focused on structure by using a timeline.

It can be seen that the authors learned the importance of a systematic procedure beginning with research of material and a chronological classification of that material in order to structure the case and make it comprehensible for the reader. The likely conclusion is that not only can structuring turn a practical case into an academic one, but also that the author's own thinking and procedures can be awakened and honed.

2.1.4 The challenge of writing a case study – significant identification of new perspectives

The composition of a case study harbours much that is new and unfamiliar, since its structure is different to that of classical academic papers which are simply divided into theory, empiricism and forecasts.

The challenge of describing the case, in addition to finding the appropriate theories, is primarily to become deeply involved with the topic. Even when one thinks one knows the case by heart, new personal perspectives on the case open up when one works to make the case comprehensible to others and uses exclusively provable time specifications as well as dealing with crucial points in a designated case-specific context. For IP 1 the theoretical part was a great challenge; for IP 4 it was particularly challenging to become deeply involved with the topic.

> IP 4: *"The challenge was to become deeply involved with a topic without knowing where the road would lead. Then another challenge was making it comprehensible to the reader. Thus things that were logical to one were often incomprehensible to an outsider. Simply to take this step back and then to describe the content in depth. To leave behind set phrases and generalisations. Thus this very intensive dealing with the content of a topic. Then to discover things which had perhaps been hidden before."*[5]

---

5   IP 4: Interview 2011, p. 2

IP 2 also sees the choice of topic as a great challenge, not only in limiting it but also in presenting the crucial points of the case. At the start IP 3 lacked a broad vision of the topic and thus failed to observe the environment.

It seems likely that through the process of composing the case study, the ability to concentrate during the writing on crucial events from one's working environment is exercised and honed. In general the following learning specifications can be determined:

- Learning that distance from the topic is necessary in order to formulate the case so that it is comprehensible to the reader.
- Learning to question theory and thus develop a feeling for which theory confirms, complements or contradicts one's own case study.

2.1.5 The "easy" parts of a case study – generating opportunities for learning

When one asks which among the challenges was especially easy for the authors, the answers range from composition of the theory section (IP 3 and IP 4) through keeping to the central theme (IP 1) to gaining access to empirical material (IP 2).

> IP 2: *"It was simple to obtain access to material. That is, because I was still working for the organisation while writing the case study and because the organisation had very sympathetically supported the work, I had de facto access to all documents which were decisively relevant and important to me."*[6]

The authors achieved different insights; these can be traced back to the nature of the case or the character of the author.

2.1.6 Learning through difficulties in writing a case study – questioning one's own competence and changing management structures

Writing a case study also harbours difficulties for the authors. For one thing, it can be difficult to present from a neutral position the various opinions from the case on a designated complex of topics or changes in management structures (IP 1). Fear of an uncertain result can resonate with the author

---

6 IP 2: Interview 2011, p. 2

(IP 4). Both the formulation of the objective presentation of the precise sequence of events in the case and the acceptance of feedback can also be difficult (IP 3).

> IP 1: *"It was especially difficult for me to address the changed management structures. It was also difficult to obtain various opinions on the complex of topics in order to draw conclusions. And it was difficult to take a truly neutral position and summarize the statements and interviews neutrally, because I also performed a key function in the case. The transition from practice to theory was also difficult."*[7]

Fear and uncertainty accompanied the case study writers. It seemed to be difficult for them to perceive these feelings and systematically to neutralise them through objectively structured procedures during the composition, with timelines and a focus on the events which actually happened.

2.1.7 Individual learning through precise observation of management decisions

In day-to-day working life one rarely finds time to grapple with closed processes or decisions which have been made in the organisation. But as the results of the interviews show, a case study offers the opportunity to deal with these. This can, furthermore, result in learning interesting new facts.

> IP 1: *"My individual learning included how to deal with a case or certain aspects within an organisational development and to illuminate a case from all sides, to recognize causes and possible effects and derive insights from them. One also gains insights for oneself from the case, since it comes from one's personal professional environment. After writing the case study I better understood certain management decisions – moving on a management level – from a management point of view."*[8]

IP 4, in contrast, recognized the strong emotional bond to the topic and learned to observe a topic precisely without the need for generalisation. Further, IP 1 commented that the case study required a certain amount of time in order to develop.

For IP 2 it was instructive to see that not everything is as it seems at first glance, but rather that one must observe many things from other perspectives and also ideally reflect on them repeatedly in order to obtain an all-encompassing view. Rather like IP 2, IP 3 also learned to observe things dif-

---

7   IP 1: Interview 2011, p. 3
8   IP 1: Interview 2011, p. 3

ferently, namely as an independent, objective observer who would simply like to have an overview of the whole.

Allowing changes of perspective, emergence of a far-reaching vision through objective methods of observation, development of the ability to reflect on one's own courses of action–these abilities enhanced the work of the interview partners on their case studies.

2.1.8 Consequences of the case study for personal development

It appears that learning is only possible by occupying oneself intensively with a topic. Thus personal development for IP 1, IP 2 and IP 3 showed itself clearly in the recognition of various methods of approach to complex processes, but also in the creation of new approaches to the working environment or increased understanding of management decisions.

IP 4 sees the potential for personal development above all through reflection on one's own function.

> IP 4: *"I experienced a very intensive involvement with my working environment and reflected on my own functions. One deals with subjects with which one otherwise has no goal in day-to-day working life; knowing or receiving confirmation that one is on the right path; not being a traditional manager but rather an advisor, a companion, and creating framework conditions."*[9]

In general, during the case studies the interview partners developed a personal maturity as well as the courage to change through dealing intensively with their own working environments, through other approaches and through reflection on their own functions.

2.2 Insights into organisational learning

2.2.1 The importance of the organisation in the case study – the support of the organisation as a condition for the success of a case study

Support from the organisation or management evidences itself primarily in willingness to make empirical material available, but also in willingness to

---

9 IP 4: Interview 2011, p. 5 and p. 6

participate in interviews (IP 4). However, regular communication between bosses and colleagues was also supportive (IP 3). IP 2 also emphasized that there was no interference by the organisation and that empirical material was available at any time.

> IP 1: *"My organisation supported me through its willingness to approve the thesis. Interviews with management and the availability of journals and draft papers to source everything were also very helpful."*[10]

Support by the organisations leads to the conclusion that they are ready to create working spaces where processes can be retraced and gone over, thus enabling learning and further development.

2.2.2 The path to organisational learning – consequences of the case study for the organisation

The question arises to what extent the organisations profit from the case studies. Of the four organisations which received case studies, in three there was no direct evidence of reactions or clear organisational learning. IP 4, in contrast, emphasized that despite a certain scepticism, the subject of learning in organisations was nevertheless accepted.

> IP 4: *"So for my boss the strong identification with the topic, with the team as such and with the topic of learning was probably noticeable."*[11]

From the findings of the interviews the conclusion can be drawn that there is a shaking up, a tendency in the direction of learning, but also scepticism in the organisations. Special consequences of the case studies for the organisations cannot be identified.

2.2.3 Learning by the organisations from the case studies

The answers to the questions about learning by the organisations from the case studies make first steps in the direction of learning visible to some extent. Thus IP 4 speaks of an aha-effect when the organisation recognized

---

10 IP 1: Interview 2011, p. 3
11 IP 4: Interview 2011, p. 7

that alongside hierarchical leadership there can also be learning and a learning organisation. IP 2 drew the conclusion that the organisation is on its way. IP 3, on the other hand, sees a type of learning in the organisation. IP 1 is not aware of learning in that sense in the organisation.

In conclusion it can be seen that the organisations which were examined are on the path to further development, or are in a learning process. The case study authors, however, feel a certain degree of uncertainty as to whether the organisations will continue down this path.

2.2.4 The path to implementation in the organisations

It is of course desirable for the insights from the case studies to be implemented in the organisations. But particularly IP 1, IP2 and IP4 do not yet want to speak of actual implementation. IP 3, however, does speak of rethinking and that individual points have actually been accepted. Incremental recognition, rethinking and acceptance of insights and changes have already been observed. The authors have located positive potential for further development in the organisations, but they do not yet speak of direct implementation.

3 Discussion and interpretation of the results

If one recapitulates how and whether individual and organisational learning due to the composition of a case study is possible, there are various results. To be able to generate learning an important basis is necessary. If one considers the recommendations in descriptions of how to write a case study, the most important relate to choice of topic. The following criteria are included:

- choosing a case from one's own working environment
- having the courage to research a case that is already completed and then to permit new insights
- identifying with the actual topic
- maintaining sufficient distance to be able to take on the role of an objective observer

Criteria can also be recognized which benefit individual learning during the composition of a case study. These include:

- interest in the academic treatment of a case
- the will to accept constructive feedback
- regular communication with colleagues

In general the following characteristics of learning can be noted – first on the level of active composition of a case study and then on the level of personal learning and development from the case study.

The learning that involves the composition of a case study can be described as follows:

- Learning that distance from the topic is necessary in order to formulate the case so that it is comprehensible to the reader.
- Learning to question theory and thus develop a feeling for which theory confirms, complements or contradicts one's own case study.

It is also evident that the composition of case studies brings with it a personal learning potential for every author, if one can perform the balancing act between personal identification and thus the emotional link to the topic and the role of an objective observer. This balancing act can be achieved if one works on the case in a structured fashion. With the help of time blocks and a focus on crucial events, space for new insights and perhaps also for individual learning can be created.

This learning can be such that not only can structuring turn a practical case into an academic one, but also the author's own thinking and procedures can be awakened and honed. In addition, decisions made in the organisation can be more comprehensible and thus better understood.

In addition, the ability to concentrate on crucial events in the working environment is practiced and honed. Possible points of individual learning also include changes in one's own perspective, emergence of a far-reaching vision through objective methods of observation, and development of the ability to reflect on one's own courses of action.

Tendencies toward willingness to learn within organisations can also be recognized. This readiness to learn is still in its infancy, since the academic method of case studies–into the bargain, written by one of the organisation's own employees–is also still new territory. In the interviews the authors speak of a shaking up, a tendency in the direction of learning, but also scepticism in the organisations. Specific verifiable consequences or further development within the organisations, which might be results of the case studies, cannot be identified

Scepticism on the part of the organisations with regard to this method, in which a completed case from the organisation is analysed in detail, is also understandable. It is clearly uncertain whether exclusively pleasant results will be generated.

Incremental recognition, rethinking and acceptance of insights and changes have already been observed. The authors located positive potential for further development in the organisations, but they do not yet speak of direct implementation.

One must certainly congratulate all these organisations for having the courage and the willingness to permit the authors to describe, examine and analyse the case studies. The space that is thus created for individual as well as for organisational learning is an important step in the direction of development of awareness of past events – independently of whether the process was positive or negative – further in the direction of development and learning.

References

Lamnek, Siegfried (2005), Qualitative Sozialforschung. Lehrbuch. 4th edition. Beltz, Basel.
Mayring, Philipp (2010), Qualitative Inhaltsanalyse. Grundlagen und Techniken.11th updated and revised edition. Beltz, Basel
IP 1 (2011): Person responsible for Public Relation and Communication. 20.8.2011
IP 2 (2011): Managing Director. 17.8.2011
IP 3 (2012): Public Relation Manager. 20.3.2012
IP 4 (2011): Head of the Marketing and the Public Relation Division. 17.8.2011

About the Authors

EVA MARIA BAUER has been a scientific employee and program director of the Center for Journalism and Communication Management at the Danube University Krems since 2003. Her working fields are communication, management and leadership, and case study writing. She developed and led two Master's programs: first "MSc Communication and Management", followed by "Communications MBA Communication and Leadership", a program for middle management which focuses on deepening and analysing skills in communication psychology, personal character building, leadership and internal communication and organisational learning. Since returning to work from maternity leave she has been responsible for the Communications MBA in Communication and Leadership, specifically for its content development, acquisition of students and external lecturers, and implementation of case studies as a research method.

Education and Certifications
- Master's degree in economics from the Vienna University of Business Studies and Economics
- Diploma as an economics trainer from the advanced training provider Corporate Consult
- University certificate as a public relations specialist from the public relations distance study program "PR+plus Austria" at the Danube University Krems
- Since September 2007 doctoral study in economics at the Vienna University of Business Studies and Economics with the dissertation topic "Misunderstandings in Organizations from a System-theoretic Perspective"

ANDREA BERGER, MA, MSc, MBA. Since April 2011 Andrea Berger has been Office Manager for Sonja Zwazl, President of the Wirtschaftskammer Niederösterreich (Economic Chamber of Lower Austria), Federal Commercial Counselor and Member of the Austrian Federal Council.
From 2004 to 2011 she was responsible for public relations and communications in a large Austrian health care organization.
Berger was head of the Press Department and spokesperson for the Christian Party of Lower Austria in St. Pölten from 2003 to 2004.
From September 2002 through May 2003 she was PR and Marketing Assistant at the Österreichischer Genossenschaftsverband (Austrian Cooperative

Association) in Vienna.
From 2000 to 2002 Berger was a freelance journalist for the NÖ Pressehaus (Lower Austrian press) in the local news section of the newspaper NÖ Nachrichten (The News of Lower Austria) and worked at the office of the editor of economic news for the same newspaper.
Education:
- 10/1997 – 04/2002
  M.A. in Journalism and Communications
  With additional courses in politics, sociology and theatre science
  University of Vienna
- 10/2007 – 06/2009
  MSc in Communication and Management
  Danube University Krems
- 09/2009 – 11/2010
  MBA in Communication and Leadership
  Danube University Krems

SILVIA ETTL-HUBER, Ph.D. (born 1970) is a scientific advisor at the Center for Journalism and Communication Management at the Danube University Krems (Austria). She studied Communication Science at the Paris Lodron University of Salzburg (Austria). She wrote her Ph.D. thesis on media marketing and later headed an international research project on the topic of media ownership in Central and Eastern Europe. She also has practical experience in the fields of advertising, media marketing, business and political communication.
E-mail: silvia.ettl-huber@donau-uni.ac.at
Danube University Krems, Dr. Karl Dorrek Str. 30, 3500 Krems, Austria.

HARALD GANSFUSS is director of finance and administration for the Central and Eastern European Branche of ASSA ABLOY Entrance Systems GmbH (automatic door systems) since 2011. He holds Master's degrees in Communication and Leadership and in Communication and Management from the Donau Universität Krems. He has over twenty years of experience in fields ranging from pharmaceuticals through metal products to automatic door systems in Austria and the Czech Republic. His management experience includes positions in controlling, sales, finance and administration.

NATASA ILIC is Expert in Marketing and Marketing Stream Leader in the Rebranding project for CEE banks at Sberbank Europe AG, Vienna (former known as Volksbank International AG). Natasa has been dealing with Marketing and Public Relations (PR) for 12 years and from 2003-2008 she was responsible for organizational implementation of Public Relations at Volksbank Serbia. Her academic background is a Master in Media & Public Relations at University Megatrend, Belgrade, Serbia and MBA in Communication and Leadership at Danube University in Krems, Austria. In her spare time, she was a journalist for several economic magazines in Belgrade. Currently she is working on a book, trying to connect her experience in the last four years (2008–2012) with the case described in the article (2003–2008). The objective is to give answers on how to become a public relations professional and develop successful and measurable integrated marketing and PR strategies.

MICHAEL ROITHER, Ph.D. (born 1978) is Head of the Center for Journalism and Communication Management and Deputy Head of the Department for Knowledge and Communication Management at the Danube University Krems (Austria). He studied Communication Science at the Paris Lodron University of Salzburg (Austria), where he majored in Journalism. He has extensive practical experience in the fields of journalism, public relations and strategic communication.

E-mail: michael.roither@donau-uni.ac.at,

Danube University Krems, Dr. Karl Dorrek Str. 30, 3500 Krems, Austria.

MARTIN STEGER is Scientific Assistant and Deputy Head at the Department of Business and Vocational Education and Training at the Johannes Kepler University Linz in Austria. His research interests concern implicit aspects of learning processes, educational theory and methodological issues as well as organisational theory, identity formation and the impact of new information technologies on the character of knowledge. Martin Steger is also engaged in education-policy topics, notably concerning teachers education. Before he started his academic career he worked as a freelancer in different consulting and conceptional contexts.

About the Authors

MARIA SPINDLER has been an organizational consultant for twenty years in economics (mainly banking and production) and at NGOs (mainly universities and foundations). Her consulting topics are strategy development, creating and changing organizations and structures, leadership culture and organizational learning. She is a lecturer at various universities on corporate culture, organization and management, and group dynamics. Her book publications deal with organizational learning, innovation, leadership, group dynamics, consulting and research. She has been qualified to train the trainer for the ÖGGO (Austrian Association for Group Dynamics & Organization Consulting) and served as board member. She holds a doctorate degree in philosophy and group dynamics.

For further information see www.maria-spindler.at.

ASTRID VALEK has been working in the banking and financial sector for 14 years. She holds a Masters degree in Public Relations and passed the Master of Business Administration (MBA) Communication and Leadership at the Danube University Krems. Since March 2012 Astrid Valek heads the Department Business Development at DenizBank AG, where she is responsible for the further expansion and growth of the bank in Europe. Before, she has been Head of Marketing & PR in Raiffeisen-bank Region Schwechat for seven years. Other stations in her business career were Skandia Austria and Deutsche Bank AG. Ms. Valek is mother of two adult sons.

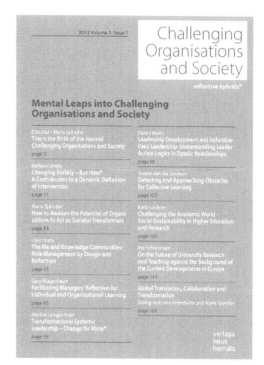

The Journal

"Challenging Organisations and Society . reflective hybrids® (COS)"

is the first journal to be dedicated to the rapidly growing requirements of reflective hybrids in our complex organizations and society of the 21st century. Its international and multidisciplinary approaches balance theory and practice and show a wide range of perspectives organized in and between organizations and society. Being global, diverse in thinking and acting outside the box are the targets for its authors and readers in management, consulting and science.

Volume 2 Issue 1, May 2013

Reflective Hybrids in Management and Consulting

Editors: Maria Spindler (AT), Gary Wagenheim (CA)

Volume 2 Issue 2, October 2013

Involving Stakeholders to Develop Change Capacity for More Effective Collaboration and Continuous Change

Editor: Tonnie van der Zouwen (NL)

Verlagshaus Hernals

WISSENSCHAFT

Maria Spindler . Martin Steger
Zwischen Universität und Unternehmen
€ 29,90, gebunden, 430 Seiten
ISBN 978-3-902744-07-4

Lisz Hirn
Friedrich Nietzsche – Die menschliche Existenz zwischen Hedonismus und Pessimismus
€ 34,90, gebunden, 144 Seiten
ISBN 978-3-9502577-9-3

Lisz Hirn
Global Humanism
Möglichkeiten und Risiken eines neuen Humanismusmodells
€ 25,90, broschiert, 64 Seiten
ISBN 978-3-9027440-8-1

Monika Öhlsaßer
Verfassungs- und Europarechtskonformität des österreichischen Glücksspielrechts
€ 45,90, gebunden, 224 Seiten
ISBN 978-3-902744-13-7

Ronald Bresich
Datenschutz und Glücksspiel
€ 39,90, broschiert, 76 Seiten
ISBN 978-3-902744-36-4

Eva Maria Gober
Schule unterm Kruckenkreuz
Erziehungsansprüche im autoritären Ständestaat Österreichs 1933/34–1938 am Beispiel burgenländischer Wirklichkeiten
€ 39,90, gebunden, 336 Seiten
ISBN 978-3-902744-10-4

Anton Grabner-Haider
Die Urkraft der Göttin
Weibliche Lebenswerte in Religion, Kultur und Gesellschaft
€ 22,90, broschiert, 150 Seiten
ISBN 978-3-902744-14-2

Anton Grabner-Haider . Lisz Hirn
Vernünftige Wege zum Glück
Ein philosophisches Arbeitsbuch
€ 22,90, broschiet, 102 Seiten
ISBN 978-3-902744-23-4